Handbook
On
Questioning
Children

A Linguistic Perspective

2nd Edition

Anne Graffam Walker, Ph.D.

ABA Center on
Children and the Law

ABA Center on Children and the Law
740 15th Street, N.W.
Washington, DC 20005

Telephone: (202) 662-1720
FAX   (202) 662-1755

The ABA Center on Children and the Law, a program of the
American Bar Association's·Young Lawyers Division, was established in 1978. Its mission is to improve the quality of life
for children through advancements in law, justice, and public
policy.

ISBN 1-57073-714-2   20978995

Legal research for this publication was performed on
Westlaw compliments of the West Group.

Table of Contents

Acknowledgements

The first edition of this book would not have been written except that Howard Davidson, Director of the Center on Children and the Law, asked me to write it; and then waited, and waited, along with my editor, Sally Small Inada – a woman of unfailing and cheerful patience– for it to get done. It would not have taken its original form if it were not for the advice, encouragement, thoughtful comments and suggestions of a number of people in addition to *Howard Davidson* who took time from their own busy lives to read, and review – on very short notice– my first draft. Those people deserve special mention. They are: *Eve V. Clark, Ph.D.*, Department of Linguistics, Stanford University; *Judge E. Preston Grissom*, Circuit Court of Chesapeake, Virginia; *Nancy E. Walker, Ph.D.*, then of the Department of Psychology, Creighton University; *Ryan Rainey*, Senior Attorney with the National Center on the Prosecution of Child Abuse; *Judge Charles B. Schudson*, Court of Appeals, Milwaukee, Wisconsin; *Suzanne M. Sgroi, M.D.*, Executive Director of the New England Clinical Associates in West Hartford, Connecticut; and *Amye R. Warren, Ph.D.*, Department of Psychology, University of Tennessee at Chatanooga.

Now, five years later, I have benefited once again from the wisdom offered not just to me, but to the fields of science and the law, by seven of my original reviewers: *Eve Clark, Howard Davidson, Judge Grissom, Judge Schudson, Suzanne Sgroi, Nancy Walker, and Amye Warren.* They were joined by another illustrious group of professionals who also managed to squeeze out a 25th hour from their days in order to read, comment on, and even move some errant commas, in the first draft of this second edition. They are *Sandra K. Hewitt, Ph.D.*, child psychologist, St. Paul, Minnesota; *Barbara R. Hoar, M.D.*, child psychiatrist, Alexandria, Virginia; *Thomas D. Lyon, Ph.D., J.D.*, The Law Center, University of Southern California; *John E.B. Myers*, McGeorge School of Law, California; *Debra A. Poole*, Department of Psychology, Central Michigan University; and *Madam Justice Marguerite Trussler, Court of Queens Bench of Alberta, Canada.*

Although the final responsibility for the opinions and presentation of information here is mine, the combined experience and expertise of these gracious professionals have made this a better book than it ever could have been otherwise.

My heartfelt appreciation to them all.

Foreword

During the past fifteen years, extraordinary attention has been focused on the way children are interviewed by social workers, police, mental health and medical professionals, attorneys, and judges. Research has enriched our knowledge of children's memory, suggestibility, and language development. Fortunately, there has been a significant increase in resources devoted to educating the thousands of professionals who interview children, and we are making progress in the effort to train interviewers. The first edition of this book was an integral part of that training effort. Now we are fortunate to have a second edition of this important work which joins two other recent publications on the "must read" list for professionals who interview children: *Investigative Interviews of Children* by Debra A. Poole and Michael E. Lamb and *Assessing Allegations of Sexual Abuse in Preschool Children: Understanding Small Voices* by Sandra K. Hewitt.

New features of the second edition of Dr. Walker's book include:
- updated references
- additional key interviewing principles
- an expanded list of basic language concepts
- further illustrative examples of the correlation between using age-appropriate language and getting accurate responses from children

Dr. Walker has also added a new chapter on the critical issue of cultural considerations in communicating with children.

The *Handbook on Questioning Children*, now revised and completely up-to-date, is one of the essential publications that mark the capstone of fifteen years of very hard work to improve interviewing of children. This book will help courts get to the truth.

John E.B. Myers
Professor of Law
University of the Pacific
McGeorge School of Law

Professor Myers is the author of *Evidence in Child Abuse and Neglect Cases* (3d ed., Aspen Law and Business, 1997).

Preface

In the five years since the publication of the original version of this book, my life has been enriched by contact with thousands of professionals from many disciplines, including the law, who work with children in the legal system. Their appreciation for the subject I teach and love – the practical application of linguistics to the critical task of communicating accurately with children – has been both rewarding and challenging. The reward comes from knowing that more and more people who question children recognize the need to learn about the significant differences in the way children and adults use and process language; the challenge comes in being presented with problems for which there is no ready and tested solution.

We have learned a lot in recent years about factors that influence children's ability to engage in sharing information with others, particularly in the artificial environment of forensic interaction. Most of that knowledge comes from the work of dedicated scholars and clinicians, some of whom have taken the time to learn about language acquisition. The rest, however, comes from the practitioners, who share with people like me their sometimes ingenious solutions to the problems they face on the job, and whose informative anecdotes give flesh to the body of scientific inquiry. It is to them that this second edition of the Handbook is dedicated.

I have written the second edition in order to add to, delete from, and update material in the first edition – notably some of the Appendices and the section on truth and lies – and to expand on information already provided, particularly the discussion of specific words and inconsistencies in children's testimony. The reader will find three added Principles, two of which – Pausing and Framing – result from my increased interest in the effect of some of the mechanics of conversation. Both of those principles have been tested empirically, and their application to increasing the amount and accuracy of information from children has proven sound. The third addition to the Principles addresses the conversational environment in which children are raised. Its application to the interview process has not, at this writing, been tested empirically; its probable relevance is based, rather, on common sense.

Common sense also led me to include a very short chapter on a few language-related cross-cultural issues that are relevant in our courts today. This has become a truly multi-cultural nation in which speakers of an astonishing array of languages typically see and judge the world based on the characteristics of the culture in which they were raised. In interactions among people who belong to the same speech community, that can be an advantage. But when the cultural and language behavior of one group is judged by the standards of another, as is the case more and more often in our courts, the result is rarely a positive one.

Having said all that, I wish the reader well, and close with the hope that the information in this book will help you reach your goal of communicating more accurately with children.

I. Introduction

In this Introduction, I want to take the personal approach, and address myself directly to everyone who picks up this book. It is, as the title indicates, a book about the linguistic complexities of questioning children, and although its primary intended readers are lawyers and judges, all interviewers of children should find it of some benefit. I have written it because I am deeply concerned by the fact that children in our courts today are being denied a right that should belong to everyone who enters the legal system: to have an equal opportunity not only to understand the language of the proceedings, but to *be understood*. This is a situation that puts not just children, but all those who stand both with and against the child, in jeopardy.

A glance at the Table of Contents may make you feel like putting this book in the stack of all the others that you intend to read someday but probably never will. So because I think that what is in this book is very important for you to know, I am going to take the somewhat unusual step of gathering together in the Introduction a few facts about children and their language that you can read quickly to get the flavor of what follows. It is my hope, of course, that at some point you will read every word, because anything you can learn that will help you level the playing field for children in our courts will eventually help level the playing field for all of us.

Some Facts About Children
To start you off, here is something that you should know. There is no doubt whatever about the following:

1. Children as young as 2 and 3 can recall and report past experience accurately (Hewitt, 1999; see Peterson, 1990, for a review)

2. Children as young as 3 have testified competently and credibly in court, (e.g., *Strickland v. State* (Alabama, 1988); *Macias v. State*, (Texas, 1989); *State v. Brovold*, (Minnesota, 1991); *State v. Ward*, (Ohio, 1992)).

3. **Even very young children can tell us what they know if we ask them the right questions in the right way.**

You will probably not be questioning children as young as 2 and 3 very often. But as children enter our court system in ever-increasing numbers, you will be seeing more and more preschool children, more school-age children, and more adolescents. This book focuses primarily on the under-10 group, but what follows is a thumbnail sketch of a few characteristics of each group. As you read through them, please keep in mind that they have been chosen not to represent weaknesses in children's ability to process adult language, but to point the way to the kind of questioning that will build on children's strengths in telling us what we need to know.

Preschoolers:

1. Use and interpret language very literally. A typical example: Asked if she could "read" an eye chart, the child responded, "No! It doesn't make words."

2. Do not handle abstractions well. Preschoolers are particularly ill-equipped to discuss with you the difference between truth and lies. They do better with concrete examples that ask them to *demonstrate* rather than *articulate* their awareness of these two very abstract concepts.

3. Aren't good at collecting things into adult-like categories. This can make it hard for them to respond to questions that ask them if "anything *like this*" happened before.

4. Use words for time, distance, kinship, size and so on, long before they understand their meaning.

5. Define words only in the simplest, action-oriented ways. A "mother" may be, "She takes care of me."

6. Have difficulty with pronoun reference. Keeping track of your "he's," "we's," "they's," "that's," and whatever it is that these pronouns refer to is not something they are good at.

7. Have difficulty with negatives. Even simple negatives like "Did*n't* you see the car?" may confuse them. "Did you *not* see the car?" is sure to.

8. *Tend* to supply a response to questions even if they have no knowledge. One reason for that is that in English, questions and answers form an indivisible pair. Answers don't happen without a question first. And if a question is left unanswered, something is perceived to be wrong. Most children learn that very early.

   The answer children supply is often (but not always) "Yes" for a number of reasons. One, in this society, it is a valued answer which indicates cooperation. Two, it is often perceived to be the one that the adult wants, particularly in response to a tag question in which the tag is negative (e.g., "You like it, *don't you*?"). And three, presented with a short restricted choice question ("Was it red *or* blue?"), children may respond to the *form* of the question, and simply reply "Yes," rather than explicitly picking one option or rejecting both.

9. Do best with simple sentences of Subject, Verb, Object. No frills.

10. Tend to focus on only one aspect of a situation or question at a time. Asking complicated questions that contain numbers of ideas is fruitless.

11. Don't organize events in their minds in an adult way. They often leave out settings, descriptions, chronology, motivations, and emotions in the telling of some past event.

12. Are still in the process of *acquiring* language. Don't be fooled by a child who sounds mature. But don't dismiss as incompetent one who doesn't seem to follow your questions. Chances are, it's the language of the question that's the problem.
13. Usually don't know that they don't understand something. So asking them, "Do you understand?" is probably a waste of breath.
14. Believe in general that adults speak the truth, are sincere, and would not trick them.

School Age, roughly 7-10:

1. Still may have difficulty in handling abstract concepts.
2. Still have problems processing complex questions and complex verb phrases that express, for instance, the future as seen from a perspective in the past (e.g., "*Were you to have been taken* to school that day?")
3. Still make errors with passives, the difference between "ask" and "tell," and with pronoun reference.
4. Are still easily confused by complex negation. Multiple negatives such as "You don't deny you did it, do you?" will probably go right over their heads.
5. Are still not mature at organizing in an adult-satisfactory way the details of narratives.
6. Are still unequipped to deal with adult insincerity such as sarcasm, irony, and so on.
7. May still believe that adults in general speak the truth.

Adolescents, roughly 11-18:

1. May or may not have acquired adult narrative skills.
2. Don't understand time as both a historical concept (one that goes on and on without them) and a day-to-day concept that affects their lives. For most adolescents, what concerns them is the here-and-now.

3. Still have difficulty with complex negation. Questions that are packed with negatives, such as "It's not untrue that you forgot, is it?" are hard to decipher. This problem continues on into adulthood for most of us.
4. Are often confused by linguistic ambiguity such as is found in newspaper headlines, some ads, metaphors, idioms, proverbs, and jokes.
5. Are likely to lose track of long, complex questions.
6. Are reluctant to ask for clarification of a question or acknowledge that they don't understand.
7. A lot of teens, particularly the under-educated, under-parented, unattached (and developmentally delayed) children remain stuck in the School Age stage above.

Although this is a book devoted primarily to alerting questioners of young children to stages of language and cognitive development that can create misunderstandings, a note might be in order here about the status of adolescents in our courts. Their linguistic and cognitive development is virtually complete, but that fact often does not work in their favor. Adults have a higher expectation of adolescents' ability to understand the convoluted language typical of court proceedings, and improbable responses to questions such as "How many times did it happen?" A: "400," are more likely to be heard as lies than as metaphors. Adolescents are, in fact, in some ways at greater risk than young children of misjudgment, and we would do well to keep that in mind.

Some Suggestions For Your Questions

And now for some suggestions for simplified questioning that will get more accurate answers from all three age groups above:

1. DO use simple, common, everyday English words and phrases. "Attorney," "Court," "deny," "subsequent,"

"take the witness stand," "at that point in time" and the like do not fall into that category.

2. DO put names and places back in where pronouns once lived. Ask, "What did Albert say?" instead of "What did *he* say?" Ask, "Were there a lot of people in the kitchen?" instead of "Were there a lot of people *there*?"

3. DO stay away from negatives. Phrase your questions positively, whenever possible.

4. DO use questions and comments that keep the number of ideas in them to a minimum. The younger the child, the smaller the number. One main idea is good.

5. DO start your questions and comments off with the main idea. "Did the bell ring when you were eating?" instead of, "When you were eating, did the bell ring?"

6. DO remember: This is a child. Children are not short adults. Try to listen to the proceedings with a child's ears. You might be surprised at what you hear.

A Final Introductory Comment

Q. Who's Tim?

A. He's my advocate.

Q. What's an advocate?

A. Someone who prays and has sex with you (Baladerian, 1993).

By taking a step too many of us fail to take – checking on the child's understanding of a word he used – this interviewer avoided the most critical error that adults make in questioning children: assuming that children use, process, and understand language in the same way we do. This is a serious mistake that can lead to 1) not formulating age-appropriate questions, 2) not properly interpreting children's responses to our questions, thereby 3) missing information that may be vital to the case, or 4) creating "information" out of a misinterpretation.

There is more, of course, to the successful questioning of children than the appropriate use of language. But language is the *essential* tool: our courts cannot function without it. And the children who come into our courts cannot function adequately without our willingness to speak *their* language. The responsibility for clear communication has to be ours. Until we accept that responsibility, until we learn how the language of children and the language of adults differ, we will not be doing our jobs as effectively, or fairly, as we can.

And now, I invite you to turn the page.

A note or two on the contents of this book.

This book is essentially a reference guide. It is organized around a set of principles that should be kept in mind during the questioning of children. Following the principles are two sections on problems to look out for in both adults' questions and children's answers. Next comes a brief section on some cultural considerations in questioning children, followed by a few language-related reasons for inconsistencies in children's testimony, and finally, the conclusion.

At the back of the book, the reader will find an updated selection from the handouts that I have been distributing over the past several years in connection with the workshops and seminars I give on questioning young children. I have called them "appendices" because they do not fit gracefully into the body of this text, but the information in them is integral to the subject of questioning children. They consist of:

- Checklist for Interviewing/Questioning Children
- A Few Suggestions for Questioning Children
- Some Basic Sentence-Building Principles for Talking to Children
- A Prototype Competency Voir Dire of Children

The appendices are in a continual process of refinement, as readers of the first edition will notice, but what appears here once again represents my best thinking at this time.

II. Principles

1. We do not question children.

We question one child at a time. Each child has his or her own unique growth pattern, and his or her own family experience which shaped the learning of language. Therefore, the child you are questioning may or may not fit the general characteristics of whatever topic is being discussed in this text. *That is markedly true in the case of children (or adults, for that matter) who have a developmental disability, come from a culture different from our own, or who have been maltreated.*

2. Language is shaped by experience.

Children pick up the words in their vocabularies first from what they see, hear, and experience around them (real-world context), and second from listening to how those words are put together in sentences (linguistic context). They learn how to use words to do things in the same way. From the people around them, they learn, for instance, what the function of questions is. "Do you want another cookie?" probably is a request for information; "Do you want another spanking?" probably is not. Children learn how they are expected to talk to adults and other children, and what counts as a tellable event and how it should be told. Not all families, even within the same socioeconomic level, and not all ethnic groups put the same value on words and how they should be used. Not all families transmit the same body of language to their children in the same way (Hall & Nagy 1979; Heath, 1983; Pease, Berko Gleason & Pan, 1993). This variability in language experience and children's expectations about how language is to be used can have a significant effect on how children respond to adults' questions. See Principle 15 for some further comments on the effects of family conversational style.

3. Children and adults do not speak the "same" language.

By the time children are about 5 years old, the language they speak sounds a lot like the one adults speak in their everyday lives. And so the assumption is made that adults and children are in fact speaking the same language. But that is not so. Language learning is far from complete at age 5. Some important aspects of grammatical knowledge are still being acquired at age 10 and even later. For example, the ability to detect ambiguity which is caused by sentence structure (e.g., Flying planes can be dangerous) develops at about age 12 (Nippold, 1988, citing Kessel, 1970). Certain communicative skills, such as giving a complete and coherent account of a personal past event, may still be developing in the late teens. Other skills which are necessary for a fully competent performance in court, such as learning how to detect and defend against reasoning flaws in other people's statements, may never be acquired even by adults.

4. Language is not an all-or-nothing affair.

Along with the mistaken assumption that adults and children speak the same language goes the assumption that once a child uses a particular word (e.g., "more") or syntactic structure (e.g., a relative clause, passive voice, negation), the child has now fully "acquired" that feature. The acquisition of language is a gradual process that often involves acquiring *parts* of a linguistic rule before acquiring the whole (Romaine, 1984). Children take a step forward (learning that the plural of "foot" is "feet") only to step back (misapplying the 's' plural to get "foots" or "feets") before moving on again (back to "feet"). Newly acquired rules, such as the use of "before"and "after," can be fragile, operating well when they are used in familiar sentence structures to talk about familiar things, but operating uncertainly in novel or stressful circumstances (French & Nelson, 1985).

5. Inconsistency in children's statements is normal.
Adults who are unaware of the nature of the language acquisition process are in danger of mistaking inconsistency in the
language of children's reports for a *fundamental* inconsistency
that would render their testimony incredible. That is unfortunate, because as noted above, from the language point of view
(and there are others), inconsistency is a normal part of the development process. The root causes of linguistic inconsistency
are discussed throughout this book, but Chapter VI addresses
some of these issues more specifically.

6. Children are very literal in their early approach to language.
The by-now classic example of the child who denies going to a
man's *house*, but later says she went to his *apartment*, illustrates
a major impediment to the credibility of children's reports:
their very narrow interpretation of meaning. Lack of experience both with language and with the world contribute to this
problem, but cognitively, the ability of young children (up to
about age 6 or 7) to move from the general (house) to the particular (apartment), and vice versa, is not well developed
(Elkind,1978). Neither is their ability – particularly for children
under 5 – to group objects and events together according to
characteristics which adults would recognize as similar. Thus,
for adults, "pants" belongs in a class called "clothes/clothing";
"touch" includes several dozen kinds of contact between animate or inanimate objects and animate or inanimate instru-
ments. But to literal-minded children, "clothes" may or may
not be recognized as including some covering for the lower
part of the body. "Touch" may be restricted to human contact
with a bare hand. For instance, one 5-year-old, when asked if
she had been touched in the shower said, No, she had just been
"washed"– on her "private, everywhere."

   Having this sort of limited range of meaning for words
keeps children from realizing that a question like, "When were
you 5?" (put to a child who responded, "I *am* 5") is seeking the
date of birth, and is not meant to imply that she cannot be five

now (A. Walker, 1987). A rigid view of agency (who does what to whom) would not, and in fact in one trial did not, allow a child to respond "Yes" to the question, "Did you ever put your mouth on Daddy's penis?" because it did not reflect the literal truth. It wasn't the *child* who did the putting, it was Daddy. *He* was the agent (Berliner & Barbieri, 1984). Since young children interpret the world based on what they themselves have seen and heard (thus the term "concrete" thinking), they are unlikely to be able to interpret a question that asks them, "What does this picture say?" since pictures can say nothing. This literal approach to language is pervasive in young and even some older children, and adults who are not aware of it can put the fact-finding process into considerable jeopardy.

7. Adult-like use of language does not necessarily reflect adult-like linguistic or cognitive capabilities.

This is another way of saying that adults and children do not speak the same language. Language and cognition do not mature simultaneously, and for that reason, children can appear to comprehend what we say, can appear to be using words and sentences in an adult way, but in reality be operating on an entirely different level. In particular, the fact that children often use words before they really understand them can deceive us as to what they are actually thinking (Clark & Clark, 1977; deVilliers & deVilliers, 1978; Copen, 1996). This is especially true with concept words which express time, duration, space, age, kinship and so on. For example, children can talk about yesterday (Q: When was yesterday? A: When I was little), and daddy (Q: Who is your daddy? What is his name? A: Name's daddy) without having any real awareness of the relationships which words of that sort represent. A more detailed discussion of this issue which once again can lead to misjudgments of a child's credibility can be found in Chapter III, Section 12.

8. Young children in particular have difficulty attending to more than one or two things at once. This includes multi-part, multi-idea questions.

"Q. Do you recall talking to her on the Sunday after they found – discovered something had happened to Doug and asking her, `Do you know Mark?' and then saying, `That is who did it'? Do you remember telling her that?" (Question asked of a 5-year-old witness during a murder trial.)

The question above is admittedly long and involved. It also is not at all unusual. The ability to answer questions like that, or any question about some event or some personal knowledge, requires the ability to keep several balls in the air at once. The question itself, once it is processed, *if* it is processed, has to be kept in working memory while the long-term memory is searched for the relevant information. Then, once the information is retrieved, it must be delivered in a way that is appropriate to and understandable by the questioner. The answer, if it is to be accurate, must also be monitored for speaker error and for misunderstanding by the listener. All of this (and more) must be done in a physical environment that may or may not be familiar, and in an emotional environment that may or may not be comfortable. In a stimulus-rich and stressful environment such as the forensic one, even adults have difficulty performing all these tasks well, as anyone who has listened to grown-ups give testimony knows. For children, the burden of doing all of these things at once may prove to be too heavy (Warren & McCloskey, 1993; Saywitz, 1995). For the very young child – given a multi-idea question – it is impossible.

It is important, then, that in the forensic environment, the questions themselves be kept *short and simple*. Remembering the question from beginning to end is, after all, the first essential task that the child has to perform. Just as with an adult, the fewer

the number of ideas there are in a question, the greater the chances are of recall, processing, and thus an accurate question/answer exchange/

9. Pausing is productive.

Pauses, whether silent or filled ("umm"), allow the brain more time to do its work. They give space to speakers for producing a thought, and to listeners for processing whatever is heard. /They also have a two-faced reputation. /In between turns, they can be deferential as the next speaker waits to be sure the first one is finished (Basso, 1972), or they can be rude by signaling a lack of involvement in the conversation (Tannen, 1985). In the legal arena, pauses between the question and the answer are seen as intelligent if the witness is your witness (Think before you speak), and as evasive if the witness is for the other side (A. Walker,1985). When a child is on the witness stand, a pause before responding gives an aggressive attorney a chance to pounce, when it should, instead, be respected as giving the child a chance to process the question – if processing it is even an option.

We talk too fast in this nation. We not only talk too fast, we tend, except perhaps in social conversations, to pack too much into what we say before we give our tongues a rest – and that's when we talk to adults. Oddly, we tend to do the same to the children whom we question in court and in court-related interviews, despite the fact that once we leave our places of work, when we talk to children we slow down. We use simpler words, shorter sentences, clearer pronunciation (Reich, 1986). We make an effort, in other words, to be understood.

Those efforts that we make outside our working world make sense. It takes children more time to process incoming signals than it does adults: for 5- to 7- year-olds, 1.9 times as long (Elliot, 1970, cited in Kail, 1991). Pausing between phrases, between sentences, and after questions gives children the processing time they need. It is a productive way to aid comprehension and achieve more accurate communication between adult and child.

10. *Children will not necessarily tell you that they don't understand you.*
One of the expectations that adults rely on in carrying on their conversations with each other is that each party will speak up if there is a perceived misunderstanding. That doesn't always happen for a number of reasons, among which is inequality of status or power. Faced with someone in authority, particularly someone who acts as if the listener ought to understand, even adults will let a misunderstanding pass by. It should not be surprising that children, who are always in a one-down position vis-à-vis adults, are often reluctant to admit that they don't understand.

But there are at least two other reasons that children may not alert adults to a lack of understanding. One, children may simply be unaware that they have the right to tell adults that they don't understand. And two, they may think that they understand a question when they in fact do not (Walker & Warren, 1995). Like adults, children will assume that they have understood an utterance if they can supply it with an interpretation. Children as old as 12 may not realize that an adult's question or statement or instruction is actually not comprehensible (Markman, 1979), either because the utterance does not contain enough information for it to be processed or acted upon adequately, or because it is marred by complex or sloppy syntax. Even college-age students have been fooled into thinking that typical lawyers' questions were easy to understand when in fact they were not (Perry, Claycomb, Tam, McAuliff, Dostal, & Flanagan, 1993). Vocabulary can also obviously contribute to misunderstanding if children believe incorrectly that their meaning and the adult's meaning for one or more of the words used is the same.

11.   *Framing is good.*

As anyone who has ever read a newspaper or textbook knows, it is easier to absorb information that has a heading over a column, or a topic line at the beginning of a paragraph or section. The information has been *framed*. We know what the subject is going to be, and knowing that, we can take in the information more quickly, more efficiently. The pump, so to speak, has been primed. And priming the pump, preparing children to respond to our questions by *letting them know what the subject is*, and *why we are asking a question*, makes good sense. It gives us one more tool for getting better information from children.

That does not mean that we must explain to a child, for instance, the reason behind our exploration of her knowledge of prepositions. It does mean, however, that we avoid precipitous topic shifts from "Do you like school?" "Yeah." to "You do. Well, that's good. Um, do you know the difference between the truth and a lie?" It means that if we are confused or want to check back on a response, we let the child in on what's going on in our heads. "I know you told me about X, but I'm a little mixed up. Would you tell me about that some more?" prepares the ground for a return to a subject, provides a frame for the topic, and may help allay the suspicion that the first answer to a repeated question was the wrong answer.

Frames do more than introduce topics and make bridges between them. They serve as a useful tool for redirecting a child's focus. In response to a child's deviation from the subject you're investigating, "O.K. We'll talk about that in a minute. Right now, let's just talk about..." is a frame that can help to keep the child grounded in the topic at hand. Making sure that you and the child are on the same page at the same time is what framing does, and it is one way to increase the reliability of the responses you get to your questions.

12. Children's responses to your questions are not necessarily answers to your questions.
A response can fail to be an answer if:

    a. it does not supply the kind and amount of information required;

    b. the parties do not agree on what the meaning of the question was;

    c. one or both of the parties fails to recognize that the question or the answer was ambiguous.

The first instance of failure to be an answer is the easiest to spot because, as a rule, it does not rely on inference. The absence or paucity or mis-match of information is explicit. For example, in the exchange, "Q. Where did you go? A. [Silence]," the requested information is missing. In "Q. Where did you go? A. Out," the information is insufficient. And there is a clear mismatch between question and answer in the exchange, "Q. Where did you go? A. Tomorrow."

But in the second and third instances listed at the beginning of this section, the fact that a response is not an answer may never be discovered, particularly if one of the parties is a child who is not yet skilled in detecting and correcting misunderstandings. In that case, inference does play a role, when, lacking any evidence to the contrary, adults assume that a child has understood the question, or when they themselves are oblivious to the ambiguity of whatever has been said or asked. Either circumstance creates difficulties for the fact-finding process. Chapters III and IV discuss this principle further.

13. The ability to recite a list is not the same as the ability to understand its contents.
As any adult knows who has to say "L,M,N,O,P" to recall which letters come before and after "O," a list is just something that sits in rote memory, more or less whole. Yet in order to gauge the competency of children, one common technique is to

get them to recite what I call our "cultural lists," all of which are learned by rote: the days of the week, months of the year, clock time, numbers, and so on. This is done in the apparent belief that if the children prove to be successful, they have the ability to respond meaningfully to questions that ask, for instance, What month, or How long ago, or How many times something happened. Children are routinely asked questions like, "You know the days of the week, don't you? So what day did this take place?"

But knowing the alphabet has little relationship to the ability to spell; counting from 1 to 10 has even less relationship to the ability to gauge the frequency of an event. As a measure of competency, then, these cultural lists merely indicate that the child has acquired the *vocabulary*. They should not be given any other significance at all.

14. Children are not born with the ability to give adult-like accounts of their personal experiences.

    Q. I see. And then you went in the shower?

    A. Yes, and then I got out and then after it was all over and then I got a ride to, to town. (Portion of an interview of a 5-year-old suspected victim of sexual abuse.)

Making the move from exclusive focus on what's happening in the present to talking about the past is one of the most important advances children make in acquiring language (Brown, 1973). But this shift is a developmental one, and as the example above shows, it is not accompanied at first by the ability to talk about past events in a way that adults in the community recognize as a narrative, or autobiographical report. That skill is a discourse skill that has to be learned.

Children apparently first learn to give autobiographical reports by responding to their parents' or other adults' questions about some past event (Hudson, Gebelt, Haviland, & Bentivegna, 1992). These questions tend at first to be yes/no questions (Eisenberg, 1985, cited in Peterson, 1990) which, as they follow one after the other, supply most of the details for the child, organize the recitation, and indicate what kind of information adults believe is significant. By asking these questions, and the more open-ended ones they ask as children grow older, adults pass on a model which they have internalized for what counts as a narrative in their community, and how it should be told.

There are six components of the model that is most widely recognized in this society: 1) a *setting* which introduces both place and players, 2) *initiating action,* 3) *central action,* 4) *motivations and goals,* 5) *internal responses* (attitudes and emotions) of the people involved, and 6) *consequences* or *conclusion.* Feeding into the model are the details that bring a narrative to life, among which are *descriptions* of sights, sounds, feelings and beliefs, and reports of what the teller and others said (Labov & Waletsky, 1967; Mandler & Johnson, 1977). The model itself is *ordered chronologically,* and it performs a dual function: it provides a structure for encoding, or remembering the event, and for recounting it later.

Children first begin to develop this model at about age 2 (Fivush, Gray, & Fromhoff, 1987), and it gradually matures as children acquire other cognitive, linguistic, and conversational skills. One essential skill is achieving control over the concept of time (see Chapter III, Section 12). Some of the other skills needed include the abilities to monitor one's own speech for error, monitor the understanding of the listener, provide appropriate pronoun reference, and use linguistic means to signal old and new information. Until *all* of these abilities are acquired – some time in the *teen years* (Labov, 1972; Whitehurst, 1976) – children's narratives tend to be incomplete and disorganized by adult standards. Incomplete narratives are harder to judge for believability, and believability is the crucial test these narratives face in the court context.

15. *Some families talk to each other; some families do not.*

That statement is an exaggeration, of course, but the conversational habits of the families children come from can differ significantly. And because those habits shape language use and understanding, they might well affect the ability of children to tell you what they know.

There are a number of viewpoints about how families can be distinguished linguistically, but one that seems particularly relevant to the forensic questioning of children focuses on their use of what Bernstein (1972) identified as restricted or elaborated codes ("code" meaning a type of speech). Perhaps an easier way to think of these families would be as "talkers" and "pointers." The codes are not mutually exclusive, but generally, families tend toward one or the other.

"Talker" families, the ones using an elaborated code, are more apt to give objects names, articulate their thoughts, and attempt to make meaning clear. They tend to be specific, and in general, make few assumptions about the listener's knowledge. "Pointer" (restricted code) families engage in less instruction with their children about the nature of objects and persons, use more pronouns, are less specific, and in their conversations, take more for granted about what the listener knows. Parents who have been identified by others (e.g., Reese & Fivush, 1993) as having a "high-elaborative" style, assist their children in recalling and recounting shared past experiences by confirming children's correct memories and using questions as prompts to help build a more complete narrative. "Low-elaborative" parents tend not to offer that kind of support, give fewer prompts, and ask the same question repeatedly in attempts to get "correct" recitations.

The effect these codes and parental styles can have on children's ability to report what they have seen was demonstrated rather neatly in a study Hawkins (cited in Bernstein, p. 167) did of two groups of British 5-year-olds. He laid out a series of pictures that told a story, then invited the children to tell the story to someone who could not see what they saw. The first of the four pictures showed some boys playing football; the second, the ball going through the window of a nearby house. Those two frames were described typically by one group as

1) Three boys are playing football and one boy kicks the ball [next picture] and it goes through the window...

and by the second group as

2) They're playing football [next picture] and he kicks it and it goes through there.

Listeners don't need to share the children's knowledge in order to understand the first story. But the second one, with its lack of specificity, would remain a mystery.

No one could expect all questioners of children to have the time or opportunity to inquire into the conversational habits of the families children come from. But these habits are not random, and they can work against children – particularly the older ones – who are not used to functioning in the elaborated code that our courts demand. Knowing that different family conversational codes and styles exist could help sharpen our listening skills, and perhaps lead to an alternative interpretation when a child seems "deliberately" vague, reticent, or remains silent in the face of our questions.

16. Familiarity matters.
In everyday living, familiarity matters. Familiarity makes it possible to concentrate on the goal, and not on how to get there. It creates expectancies (Brown & Lennenberg, 1958) about events and people, and it supplies a base from which we

can conduct our behavior, infer intention, and forecast the future/ Familiarity can be a help if we infer correctly, but a hindrance if we are wrong.|And what is familiar depends on experience.

In language, familiarity matters too, and is a particularly critical factor with children. For instance, when preschool children talk about familiar, everyday events, they are usually accurate in their use of grammatical terms to express temporal (e.g., "before"), causal (e.g., "because"), and logical relations (e.g., "or," if"). They are not as successful, however, when they attempt to describe experiences they have never had before (French & Nelson, 1985).

Familiarity even conditions a child's response to a question. As noted in Principle 15, not all families use questions to accomplish the same ends (Heath, 1983), and although children learn to modify family expectations when they enter school, nothing in any of their everyday environments is likely to prepare them to meet the expectations held by adults who ask children questions in court or in forensic interviews of any kind.

One final note here on the relevance of familiarity issues to children's testimony. A growing body of research suggests that children are more accurate and complete in their responses to evidentiary questions when they have been familiarized with the questioner, the setting, the language, and the customs of the legal world they are about to enter (Saywitz & Snyder, 1993; Saywitz, et al., 1993). This is a finding worth paying attention to by anyone who is interested in increased comprehension, accuracy, and completeness of children's reports in legal contexts.

17. Culture matters too.
The children who come into our courts are an increasingly diverse group. Some of the diversity is easily marked: different

attire, different color skin, hair type, eye or nose or lip shape. Some of it is not: a child who has grown up on a diet of T.V. may look a lot like the one who loves books. Probably most of the children you see will speak English; an increasing number will not. Other children, those who come from other countries, may *speak* English, but have even less ability to comprehend and to cope in a forensic setting, than will a native child of the same age. *The temptation to rely upon such children to act as translators for their siblings or parents in any kind of interview with forensic implications should be firmly resisted.*

But no matter what language the children who enter the courts have, the tendency is to believe that they all *learned* language the same way, that their nonverbal means of expression are basically the same, and that what counts as a story to one counts as a story for all. Unless we are aware of cultural differences, it is tempting to believe that the chief function of questions for everyone is to gain information, that silence is often not golden, but bad, and that families are families everywhere. We not only tend to believe these things, we react to the children as if they were true.

So if a child lowers her head and does not look us in the eyes when she tells us what happened, we may think she is lying, instead of looking to her culture, which might dictate that behavior as an expression of respect. If a school-age child cannot get to the point in a narrative, we may believe that he cannot follow directions, is perhaps not too bright, or is being evasive, unless we know that in his culture, his loosely chained series of topics, strung together in no particular order, is the acceptable form that stories take (Michaels & Collins, 1984). When children of all descriptions do not seem to be able to answer questions the way our *own* children do, we are not apt to think about the fact that in some cultures, questions are not to be "answered" as much as they are to be obeyed as an order or to be absorbed as models of how to see the world ("Isn't that beautiful?"). If anyone, anywhere, responds to a question, or statement, with what we consider a significant pause, we treat that silence as something gone wrong (A. Walker,1985). And when children from cultures other than our own talk about their "mothers," "fathers," "brothers," "sisters," "cousins," "aunts," "uncles," and "grandparents," we give those terms the same values we have. In each one of these instances that can matter in how children's testimony is judged, we might very well be wrong. These issues, as well as those discussed in Principles 15 and 16, are taken up in somewhat more detail in Chapter V.

18. Even very young children can be competent witnesses in a court of law.

This last principle is not strictly a linguistic one: many factors other than language enter into consideration of children as witnesses in a court of law. But as research into evidentiary interviews with children shows (e.g., Brennan & Brennan, 1988; Lyon & Saywitz, 1999; Perry, et al., 1993; A. Walker, 1993; Poole & Lamb, 1998; A. Walker, 1999), language can be a barrier between the child, the adult, and the truth. It need not be: even very young children have the competence to tell adults what they know when they are questioned in age-appropriate ways that allow for the still-developing state of children's cognitive and linguistic skills (Hewitt, 1999; Perry, 1995; Perry and Wrightsman, 1991; Saywitz, Snyder, and Lamphear, 1996). Until those skills have fully matured at some point in the mid teens, the responsibility for getting at what children know rests *squarely on the adult*, and in particular, on the language of the question, and not on the language of the answer.

III. Problems to look out for in your questioning

The goal of evidentiary questions should be to get accurate answers, but that goal is unlikely to be reached if the questions can't be understood. Evidence that children don't understand a great many of the questions they are asked in court-related contexts has already been well established through analysis of actual court transcripts (e.g., Brennan & Brennan, 1988; Carter, 1992; A. Walker, 1987, 1993). There have been, however, two studies to date in which children's understanding was actually *tested* by measuring their *ability to answer* some typical questions they face in court. The results of those studies, which, taken together, included children from preschool through college age, provided empirical evidence that "lawyerese" can be dangerous to our judicial health (Perry, et al., 1993; Peters& Nunez, 1999).

Among the several problems characterized as lawyerese by the Perry, et al. 1993 study were the use of difficult vocabulary and complex questions. These and other problems associated with court questioning are taken up in Sections 4 through 19 below. Sections 1 through 3 provide an early warning system on other words and word classes that are often critical in evidentiary contexts, but that can also contribute to misunderstandings between adult and child in everyday life.

1. Prepositions.
Prepositions seem like such simple words that it is easy to overlook them as potential troublemakers, yet command of them is essential in order to talk accurately about "where." Children begin to use prepositions at about age 1-and-a- half to 2, and most, but not all, prepositions are acquired by the time

children are about 5-and-a-half (Clark & Clark, 1977). During that learning period, however, children make mistakes. Three-year-olds, for instance, can use "in" to mean "between," and "on" for "above" (Clark & Clark, 1977). Four-year-olds can mix up "above," "below," "at the bottom of," and "in front of," which is a preposition that can be interpreted in different ways even by adults (A. Walker, n.d., unpublished research). The words "before" and "after," which are often used as preposi-tions (e.g., "before lunch," "after dinner") can present particu-lar problems for preschoolers, and as conjunctions, may still not be mastered by *native* English-speakers at the age of 6-and-a-half (Reich, 1986, citing Tibbits, 1980). See paragraph 3 below, and Chapter V, Section 2 for further discussion.

2. Pronouns and other pointing words that have nothing close by to refer to.
Another kind of word that adults use without thinking at all are deictic words, also called indexicals (you can think of them as an index finger, pointing at something). The most familiar indexicals are the pronouns, such as "I," "him," and "that," but words like "here," and "come" also fall into this class. The problem with these words is that they are inherently ambigu-ous: their meaning depends entirely on whoever uses them. For instance, "I" can only be used by a speaker; "he" can only refer to someone else. "Here" can be understood only by knowing where the speaker is; words like "it" and "that" have no meaning at all unless they refer to something else.

Being able to use these "pointing words" accurately requires the abilities to understand speech roles, how people fit into them (Charney, 1980), and how to gauge what the listener knows (Pease, et al., 1993). To some extent, children have these basic capabilities when they are 3 and 4 years old (de Villiers & deVilliers, 1974), but gaining full mastery of the use of indexicals is a slow process. For example, understanding that certain pairs of them *contrast* with each other (e.g., "this/that"; "here/there") comes at about 5 or 6. Mastery of pairs like "come/go" and "bring/take" is apparently not acquired by some children until they are 7 or 8 (Clark & Garnica, 1974). And firm control of pronouns that come before the object referred to ("When *he* got to school, was *John* late?") – that is, understanding that the pronoun and the *following* noun refer to the same person – may not come until the middle school years (Tager-Flusberg, 1993; Wigglesworth, 1990).

Keeping track of these indexical words, either within one question ("*He* showed you on *his* head where *he* was hurt, didn't *he*?", referring to two different people), or across a series of questions, can be very difficult even for adults. It can be especially difficult for children who have so many other tasks to attend to in an interview situation. All of these problems can result in misunderstandings, which in turn can affect perception of a child's credibility. The solution to the problems, however, is rather simple: Keep questions short, replace indexicals frequently with specific nouns ("Steve" instead of "he," "in the back yard" instead of "there"), and make an explicit check now and then to be sure both child and adult are talking about the same thing. See also Chapter IV, Section 2.

An added caution: Young children can be tricked by external attributes such as hairstyles, unusual facial hair, or clothing (and costumes), into misidentifying a girl as a boy, a man as a woman or vice versa, so may use the wrong pronoun in connection with that person (Wood, 1981, p.133). Such confusion could well contribute to diminishing a child's credibility unfairly.

3. Some specific words:

ahead of/behind. These words can be used to talk about both space and time. It's a good idea to avoid using them entirely with children under 7 when referring to time. (One study by Richards (1982) showed a zero comprehension rate for 5-year-olds). They should be used cautiously with children under 6 when talking about space ("Was she walking behind you?").

always/never. These absolutes are generally acquired by children by age 5 (Siegal, 1991), but they are heard both before that age and long after during truth/lie competency questioning: "Do you always tell the truth?", "And you never tell a lie?" Those questions in themselves tempt an incorrect answer even from adults, but for preschoolers, they can be particularly dangerous (see Section 13 below). Research has shown that some of these young children make no distinction between the words "always" and "never," interpreting them as a pair which is either positive or negative (deVilliers and deVilliers, 1978, citing Kuczaj, 1975). Whether the children you question are in that stage or not, absolutes such as "always" and "never" – as well as the words "any" and "ever" – require making a careful search through all past experience in order to answer accurately. Adults can have difficulty with that cognitive operation; it is unreasonable to expect children to succeed where grown-ups fail.

any. Answering a question that includes the word "any" or its compounds (e.g., "anything," "anyone," "anywhere") generally requires making a global search through all possibilities, something even adults fail to do if their memories are not jogged. It is non-specific enough that it regularly generates inconsistent answers, such as the frequently inaccurate "No" response to the questions, often posed in sexual abuse cases, "Did anything happen?", and "Did he/she say anything to you?" With both adults and children, an "any" question can generate a "No," followed immediately by information that contradicts the negative ("Was anyone there?" "No, just Sam.")

One explanation for that inconsistency is that in English, the word "any" has a negative polarity in contrast to the more neutral or positive, "some." That is, "any" is more closely associated with negatives than is "some": "He did*n't* give her *any* (not 'some') presents," as opposed to "He gave her *some* (not 'any') presents.") (Quirk, Greenbaum, Leech, &

Swartik, 1985). This negative "push," which is a *trend* only, may account for the findings of my research on naturally oc-curring speech (as opposed to speech elicited in laboratory studies). Those findings suggest that questions that include the words "any," (as well as compounds such as "anyone," "anything," "anywhere") are more likely to trigger a nega-tive response which is inaccurate ("Did you have anything to eat?" "No, just a sandwich") than are questions which use the word "some." Some clinicians have also noted infor-mally that "anyone" (and "someone") can be perceived by very young children as if it were a specific person's name, thereby guaranteeing that the answer to "Did you see Any-one?" will be "No."

ask/tell. The meaning difference in these words is often not sorted out by children until they are anywhere from 7 to 10 (Kessel, 1970, Chomsky, 1969). One reason may be because "ask" has the dual meaning of both a question ("He asked her what to wear") and a polite command ("I asked you to sit down"). This confusion can also lead to misinterpretation of a child's answer, if the child is thinking "command" and the adult is thinking "invitation" ("Did she ask you to come over?").

before/after. When these words are used to indicate time, they show up in children's speech long before the children have mastered the rules for their use (probably by age 7: Reich, 1986). Even at a young age, children can use them accurately when they talk about events that are familiar to them, but when they attempt to describe unfamiliar events, or are *ques-tioned* about an event, they can mix up the two. This is par-ticularly likely to happen if the words are not used to match the actual order of events they describe. A question that asks, for example, "Did you tell your mom before you ate dinner?" matches the order of events. "Before you ate din-ner, did you tell your mom?" does not.

Answers to these questions are more likely to be accurate if they reflect the order of the event; otherwise, especially with children 5 and under, they may simply reflect *whether* the child told mom, and not when (Clark & Clark, 1977; French & Nelson, 1985). Of the two words (which may be conjunctions and adverbs as well as prepositions), "after" may be acquired a bit later than "before" by native speakers of English (Clark, 1971; Goodz, 1982). Anecdotal evidence (which must not be mistaken for evidence from scientific studies) from the Hispanic community suggests that command of these two English words may come as late as age 14 or 15 for children whose native language is Spanish and who are speaking English as a second language. (See also Chapter V, Section 2, and Chapter VI, Sections 4 and 5.)

Note: The word "before" should *never* be used with children to indicate a spatial relationship: "You appeared/came *before* the court"..."You stand now *before* the court."

big. Just for a moment, try an experiment. Pretend that you are demonstrating to someone who is learning English what "big" means. Where were your arms? Spread wide to the side? Held high over your head? Curved out in front of you? How would you have shown what a "big" load was? Did you consider the meaning of "big" as in "big sister," or "big" as in adult, not child? All of those meanings – broad, tall, fat, heavy, older, grown-up – are possible when a young child describes someone as "big." The answer, then, to a question like "Is she bigger than me?" is ambiguous at best, especially since the ability to compare the size, height, weight, age and other physical attributes of someone who is not present is problematic not only for children, but for many adults. Asking a child if an object was big is equally problematic. What is small to us may be big to a child, particularly if it is an object that was used in an abusive or threatening way.

different/same. "Different" means "not the same," but "same" can mean either "identical," or "similar," and it is risky to assume that children under 5 have mastered any of those distinctions. Asked to play with the "same" toy she had just put down, a 3-year-old is just as likely to pick up one nearby that is the same kind (similar) as she is to choose the original (identical) plaything. By age 5 or 6, children make that kind of differentiation comfortably (Wood, 1981, citing Karmiloff-Smith 1977). It may take another three or four years, however, before children are able to recognize that things that seem generally *similar* have to be identified as *different* if they have even the slightest variation (Poole & Lindsay, 1995, citing Vurpillot & Ball, 1979). See also Chapter III, Section 13 on the important application of "difference" to questions on truth and lies.

forget. For adults, "forget" generally means one of two things: a lapse in memory, as in "I've forgotten her name," or a failure to carry out an intention, as in "I forgot to buy the milk." It can be used conversationally in other ways that have nothing to do with either prior knowledge or intention ("Don't forget to take your lunch"); but when a child answers a question with "I forget," we aren't thinking in terms of "conversation." We may be thinking "uncooperative" or "obstinate," but more likely, we're thinking "failure." The child is saying that he failed to recall something he once knew. And that is highly probable: children of normal development generally acquire that "I knew it once but don't know now" meaning of "forget" at about age 4 (Lyon & Flavell, 1994). But if we're talking with children 7 and under, the younger the child, the more likely it is that they could be thinking in quite different terms – that of not ever having known, or perhaps of failing to carry out an intention – meaning differences which could be significant in a forensic environment (Wellman & Johnson, 1979; Hill, Collis, & Lewis,1997).

first/last. Children begin to use "first" before they are quite 3 years old (French & Nelson, 1985), and with preschoolers, it seems to be easier to get accurate responses when "first" is used instead of "before." But even 5-year-olds still make comprehension mistakes with both these terms (Richards, 1982), even though they use them fluently in talking spontaneously about familiar events (French & Nelson, 1985).

inside. In sex abuse cases involving suspected penetration, many jurisdictions require that a child be asked if an

offending object or body part has been inserted "inside"one
of his or her orifices: mouth/vagina/anus. Sometimes,
again depending on the jurisdiction, that question is expanded to include "how far."   Getting an accurate response
to either question requires the following: 1) the skill of the
questioner in asking the question in an age-appropriate way;
2) the child's full command of the preposition "inside";
3) awareness of how many, what, and where the critical orifices are; 4) what exactly "inside" the body means; and most
problematic of all, 5) a child's *perception* of what "inside"
means in relation to whatever incident is being discussed.

Unfortunately, my experience thus far both in teaching and
in research indicates that most interviewers, including attorneys, rarely check on acquisition of prepositions of any kind.
If they do check, they are troubled as to the best way to determine what "inside" a *body* means, and seem to overlook
the problem of perception completely. Yet for young children in particular, anything between the legs can be perceived as "inside"; young female children have a special
problem dealing with that question because of their anat-
omy. They do not know, and have no reason to know, that
they have a vagina in addition to the other two openings.
And as to "how far," penetration of any degree can feel like
too far – and no doubt it is.

know/think/guess/sure. These terms are used in a conversational
way by children as young as 2-and-a-half (Olson &
Astington, 1986) ("Know what? I got some candy."), but they
do not begin to reflect the appropriate mental processes until
children are about 4 years old (Moore & Furrow, 1991;
Abbeduto & Rosenberg, 1985). When the word "know" is
used to ask them about their own state of knowledge ("Do
you know who Mr. X is?"), children can respond quite accurately by about age 5 (Mitchell & Robinson, 1992). These
terms, however, are often used by adults to express different
degrees of *certainty* rather than knowledge. The studies show
that at about age 4, children begin to place more weight on
knowing and being sure than on thinking or guessing

(Moore & Furrow, 1991), but it is not until they reach 9 years of age that they use them reliably in that sense. (The Moore and Furrow study showed that even adults make an uncertain distinction between "think"and "guess.") Consequently, using them to distinguish the certainty of children's knowledge ("Do you know that, or do you just think that?") may lead to inaccurate and/or inconsistent answers.

let/make. "Let" implies permission; "make" implies coercion ("She let me do it"; "She made me do it"). Preschoolers can mix up these two words (Bowerman, 1988).

more/less. The word "more" is an early word for children, but when it first appears, it simply means a repetition ([I want] More milk.) Its comparative sense is apparently not acquired until children are about 6 years old, (Reich, 1986), particularly when "more," a high frequency word, is used in contrast with the word "less," a very low frequency word. Asking a question like, "Was it more or less like/than/" etc. with children much under 10 is probably not wise. Asking a preschooler a question such as, "Had you spent more than one night at your granny's house" is not just unwise, it is futile.

move. There is not much published research on children's understanding of this word, but anecdotally, in the field of sexual abuse, it would appear that even some 7-year-olds do not have a clear idea of what it means, for example, for a penis to "move." That may be because "move" is a higher order word, one like "touch," that has a wide range of meaning. Higher order words (see Chapter VI, Section 7) are more abstract, so it is not surprising that children who think in terms of lower order words, such as "wiggle," "poke," or "push/pull," and who are not skilled at manipulating abstract concepts, have difficulty with this word.

neither/either, another, each. These terms are called "quantifiers" – words we use to talk about sets of things – and they are used all the time in questions we put to children: "Did *either/neither* of you get hurt?" "Did she give *each* of you a present?"; "Was there *another* person there?"   As ordinary as they are to us, they can be difficult for young children to process accurately. In one study, only about half of a group of children aged 4 to 7 were able to follow directions which used the words "another" and "either." Fewer still could use the word "neither" appropriately, and depending on the difficulty of the task they were asked to carry out, the rate of success in understanding "each" ran from 31 percent to a startlingly small 3 percent (Hanlon, cited in Kessel,1988).

There can be considerable danger in applying experimental findings to real-world situations, particularly if the laboratory studies have not been done on the kind of population to which those findings are being applied. But it is worth noting that this group of children had difficulty in processing these words in a concrete task in which they were manipulating objects they could see and feel. That suggests an increased level of difficulty when adults use quantifiers to ask non-task related questions about people and events in the past. It might be wise, then, particularly with preschoolers, to be cautious about using this group of problematic words. Given a proper prior foundation, open-ended questions such as "Who got hurt?" and "Who got a present?" might result in more accurate responses. They not only avoid quantifiers, but by avoiding the Yes/No question form, they allow the information to come from the child. (See also the sections on "any", and "some/all," which are also quantifiers.)

promise. From a strictly linguistic perspective, "promise" is a tricky verb in English, because it violates a basic grammatical rule – the Minimum Distance Principle (MDP) – which states that the subject of a verb in a complement phrase is the noun closest to, and in front of, that verb (Chomsky, 1969). As an illustration of how the principle works, consider that in each of the following questions, "Do you want *me to sing*?", (complement phrase is italicized) and "Would you tell *me to sing?*", the prospective singer is the speaker "me," the noun right in front of the verb "to sing." However, in the common court question, "Will you promise *me to tell the truth*?", the rules change. The prospective truth-teller is now the *hearer* "you," the noun in front of both the main verb "promise" *and* of the infinitive verb phrase "to tell the truth." Adults understand this violation of the MDP without thinking. But children up to the age of 10 may not (Chomsky, 1969), which can result in exchanges like the following one between an interviewer and 10-year-old child:

Q: Promise me to tell the truth.

A: I'm sure you will! (Richardson, 1989).

It is important to emphasize that the difficulty that this example represents is with the *use* of the word "promise" in a sentence, and not with the concept. Grammatical misunderstandings of this type can be avoided in competency questioning either by making sure that with older children, there is only one pronoun preceding "promise" ("Do *you*/ Will *you*) promise to tell the truth?") and with pre-schoolers, either that all of the grammatical markers are left in ("Do you promise *me that you will* tell the truth?"), or that reference to the speaker ("me) is left out ("Do you promise you will tell the truth?"). Incorporating the word "will" might be an especially good idea with children under 7, who seem to regard it as placing a stronger obligation on them to tell the truth than does the word "promise" alone (Lyon, Kaplan, Dorado,& Saywitz, 1999).

Although the word "promise"' is associated most closely in court proceedings with truth-telling, it can be used in other ways that are difficult for young persons to process. One use that can be a problem even for school-age children is found in the question that some judges feel they must ask: "Has anyone promised you anything for coming here today?" That wording uses a somewhat advanced verb form ('has promised'), and leaves out the essential phrase 'to give' (promised *to give* you). If such a question is necessary, it might be better to avoid the use of "promise" altogether by asking something like, "Did someone tell you that you'd get [a treat/something special/to do something fun...] for coming here today?" Chapter III, Section 13 elaborates further on this problematic word.

remember. Most adults would probably say that you need to have prior knowledge of something in order to remember it, and that the "something" actually has to have existed, or have happened. The prior knowledge, in other words, has to be a "fact." While children as young as 4 years old have shown an awareness of this factive characteristic of "remember" (Abbeduto & Rosenberg, 1985), studies suggest that an adult-like understanding of this word may not be reached until children are about 8 or 9 years old (Abbeduto & Rosenberg, 1985; Johnson & Wellman, 1980; Saywitz, Jaenicke, & Camparo, 1990). It is possible, for example, for a child to believe that to remember, one must first *forget*, a belief expressed by a preschooler who explained, when asked why he said he didn't remember an event that he had participated in, "Because I didn't forget yet, so I still know it." (Sandra Portko, personal communication). Such a belief, if not discovered, could obviously cause highly misleading responses which would not reflect a child's real knowledge.

some/all. Children use these words from the time they are about 2 years old, but as with the pair "more/less," they don't fully reach adult skills in using them contrastively until they are about 6 or 7. Nor do they necessarily realize that the word "all" can include the meaning of the word "some." One 6-year-old who could read, denied that he knew *some* of the alphabet, because, as he explained vehemently, "I know *all* of it." (Beck, 1982).

touch. In cases involving sex abuse, "touch" is a word that has special significance, so it is particularly important that questioners recognize it as one of those "higher order" words that adults understand to include many kinds of contact, but that children may understand to mean one specific kind of contact with one specific kind of instrument (as with the hand). A child as old as 6 may deny being touched, but later talk about something being "put in" his mouth. *An act does not cease to be an act if the words used to describe it are not mutually understood;* nor does it become a lie. The challenge is to recognize the limitations of word meanings for children, and to craft questions that get at those limitations. Children recognize the words "hit," "kiss," "hug," "pat,"  "smack/spank," and many other simple words that involve touching. Asking if the child gets kisses, for instance, who kisses him, and where, is one way to move from the specific to the general ("touch") in a non-suggestive way that may lead to better communication of the facts. See Hewitt, 1999 for an excellent discussion of "touch."

Yesterday/today/tomorrow. To use these three words accurately, children must learn that they do not refer to any particular day of the week (e.g.,Tuesday), but refer instead *only* to the specific day before, the day of, or the day after the day on which they are spoken (deVilliers and deVilliers, 1978, p.121). Thus, if one is speaking on Wednesday, Monday cannot be yesterday, and Friday cannot be tomorrow. The only one of these three time words that young children use correctly – and not always – is "today." When "yesterday" is used accurately by preschoolers, it is probably coincidental, because to them that term includes anything that happened in the past (Peterson, 1990). "Tomorrow" simply refers to something that hasn't gotten here yet. Although there are always exceptions, expecting even 6-year-olds to have wrapped their minds around the fact that in English, these words represent blocks of time which are strictly defined in terms of when they are spoken, is unrealistic. It pays to find out what children's understanding of these time words is if either you or they talk about "yesterday" and "tomorrow." (But see Section 14 below on checking children's understanding.)

4. Legalese.

People who enter a foreign country are not expected to understand the language. But both adults and children who enter the legal world are expected to understand and respond knowingly to its language, much of which is as foreign to them as Urdu is to most readers of this text. A sample of the kind of language which studies have shown to cause incomprehension, which in turn renders the question/answer process problematic at best, follows. (See Saywitz, 1989; Saywitz, et al., 1990 and Warren-Leubecker, Tate, Hinton, & Ozbek, 1989 for a thorough discussion.) All of the following words and phrases have been used in questions put to children as young as 4 years old, and every one of them could be simplified or eliminated altogether without jeopardizing in any way the search for the truth. No word that cannot be clearly explained should ever be used in questioning a child.

Legal words. Allegation, appear, attorney, court (in reference to the judge), counsel, defendant, evidence, hearing/preliminary hearing, jury, minor, motion, oath, parties, perpetrator, prosecutor, statement, testify, witness ...

Latinate words. Admit, allegedly, apprehend, approach, area, consequences, deny, describe, depict, differentiate, engage, exaggerate, experience(d), figment (of your imagination), incident, identify, indicate, insert, interfere, located, matter, occasion, occurrence, prior to, recall, recollect, reference/with reference to, regarding/as regards, reside, respect (with respect to), scene, sequence, sincere, subsequent ...

Jargon. Expressions: I submit/suggest/put it to you that; What if anything; Who if anyone; Where if anyplace; Did there come a time; Did you appear before the court; Take an oath; Tell these ladies and gentlemen and His Honor; Take the witness stand ...

Pomposity. During that time span; Was it then necessary; On this particular visit; When you next saw it; At this/that point in time; Was that not true; And did you know it to be...

5. Complex sentences

What makes a complex sentence complex? Most people would prob- ably answer "length" to that ques- tion, and length can certainly be a factor, but the correct answer is anything that increases processing time. All of the following have been shown in studies of *adult* com- prehension to make understanding a sentence more difficult. It should be noted that each one of these fac-

tors was studied *separately*; combining them obviously adds to the difficulty. It makes sense, then, to avoid them when talking to children. That is what adults do, in fact, in their daily lives: modify their language so that children can understand what they say. There doesn't seem to be any justifiable reason why it cannot also be done in court, particularly since the stakes are so much higher, and children are far less likely than adults to admit, or even to recognize, a lack of comprehension. In one study, children ages 5-1/2 to 7-1/2 asked for clarification of only *1 percent* of the complex questions they were asked (Carter, Bottoms, & Levine, 1996). It should come as no sur- prise that responses to such questions tend to be inaccurate.

a. *Abstract and low frequency words*. Words that express ab- stract concepts rather than concrete ones (e.g., "area" v. "back yard"; "truth" v. "what's real"), are both harder to understand and to recall, and the same is true of low fre- quency words such as "empty," "few," "less," "narrow." (See Felker, 1980 for a review.) Abstractions of any kind are beyond the grasp of most children who are younger than 6 or 7 (Elkind, 1978) and not until they reach the age of about 11 at the earliest, can they be expected to approach the kind of abstract, hypothetical reasoning so many court questions require (Perry & Teply, 1985, cit- ing others).

b. *Ambiguity.* Adults have acquired enough experience with both language and the world to know that not just words ("bank"), but sentences ("John has painted furniture"), utterances ("It's cold in here"), and events (being asked the same question twice) can be interpreted in more than one way. Very young children should not be expected to have any of this knowledge; by the age of 12, normally developing children can probably be expected to be aware of all of these kinds of ambiguity, but to a limited degree (Kessel, 1970). Children's ability to apply their knowledge, of course, depends on their exposure to new words and ways of using them. Until age 18 or 19, some kinds of linguistic ambiguity can remain challenging for children, particularly for those who do not have high intelligence or a reflective problem-solving style (Nippold, 1988). Even adults, who typically have the ability to recognize ambiguity in all its forms, frequently fail to do so, particularly in connection with certain prepositional phrases (e.g., "in front of") and inherently ambiguous words like pronouns. (A. Walker, n.d., unpublished research). See this chapter, Sections 2 (Pronouns) and 8 (DUR/X Questions) for additional examples of ambiguity. ·

c. *Embedding.* Embedding involves putting potential sentences inside a sentence. An example of a simple embedding is "The news that *he had written a play* surprised everyone." Nominalizations (see below) are also a kind of embedding. "I remember *telling* you that before," turns "that I told" into one word, and buries it inside another sentence. Embeddings, particularly if there are a lot of them, and if they occur somewhere other than at the end of a Subject-Verb-Object sequence, make sentences (like this one) harder to process. One common type of embedded structure is the relative clause – signaled by words like "who," "where," "which," and "that" – which tells us something about the word it follows ("The <u>house</u> *where I live...*).

By the age of 4, children are already producing relative clauses (That's the one *[that] I want*). However, until they are in school, they can't keep track of them very well, particularly if there is more than one, and if the clause comes anywhere but at the end of a short sentence. Even after children have reached first and second grade, it is wise to keep relative clauses, and other types of embedding, to a minimum.

d. *Left-branching*. The sentence which English speakers are most accustomed to hearing sounds something like this: "The dog ate my homework." That is, the favored form of sentence in the English language is right-branching: it begins with the Subject (The dog), moves right toward the Verb (ate), and moves right again toward the Object (my homework). That is the form that children first acquire, and the form that is easiest to process. Sentences which put something in front of the Subject (*"Although I probably could've come up with a better excuse, the fact is that the dog ate my homework"*), are classified as left-branching. Left-branching creates complexity because it often involves embedding (see paragraph c above) and puts a strain on short-term memory. While most of the things said in everyday life begin with Subject-Verb, a great many trial and pre-trial utterances do not.

One very easy way to increase young children's comprehension of statements is to return to everyday forms: keep the subject and main verb together, and put them both at the beginning of the sentence. The same techniques can be used with questions. To keep them as simple as possible, first, avoid "front-loading" a question (*"On the night of July 5th when you saw your dad again for the first time*, did your mom say anything?"). And second, even though questions differ in syntactic form from statements, it is still a good idea to keep the three main, Subject-Verb-Object components in questions as close together as possible. "*Did you cry* when you fell down?" is easier to process than *"Did you,* when you fell down, *cry*?"; *"What did you do* after school?" keeps the components closer together than *"What,* after school, *did you do*?"

e. *Negation*. Questions that have negatives in them are popular in adversarial exchanges such as cross examination, but they are not reliable tools for getting accurate information from either child or adult. As any school teacher knows, negative questions are more apt to be misinterpreted on a test, and the answers are far less likely to be accurate than if they were framed positively. The Perry, et al., study (1993), for example, found that children on average (including kindergarten through college-age students) gave correct answers only 50% of the time at best to questions that had either single ("Did you not see a woman in the video?") or double negatives in them ("Is it not true that Sam did not knock over the blocks?"). Significantly, when those same questions were posed *without* the negatives, the children answered them correctly 70 –100% of the time.

It might be helpful to understand three underlying reasons for why negation can be so troublesome. First, to get to "not X," you must first know what "X" is. Second, there are at least three kinds of negation. *Syntactic* negation is the easiest to spot when the words "not," "no," and "never" appear in the sentence (e.g., "It is *not* green"). *Morphological* negation is signaled by a prefix which negates the word it is attached to (e.g., *un*responsive, *ir*relevant, *dis*satisfied). And *semantic* negation hides within the meaning of a word (e.g., forget, deny, miserable, empty, hardly, except, unless). The third reason that negation can cause trouble in comprehension is fairly obvious: the more *kinds* and the more *instances* of negation there are in one sentence, the harder it is to process. "Oregon is north of California" is easy to understand. "California is not north of Oregon" is harder. "Do you deny that it isn't incorrect to say that Oregon is not south of California?" needs pen and paper and time to figure out.

 Multiple negatives, however, are not responsible for the only problem that children face when they are asked a negative question. Their strategies for processing them still are not in place at age 9. One example: given a sentence like, "You could see that he was *not* home," children up to that age can interpret it to mean, "You could NOT see that he was at home," transferring the negative to the clause that came first (Phinney, 1981), thus changing the facts completely. Such a strategy could lead to answers that give no indication of a child's actual knowledge. It is probably a wise course, then, to keep negatives in questions, like other complicating factors, to a minimum, and to be especially alert to the implications of asking them.

f. *Nominalizations.* The most common kind of a nominalization is one that changes a verb into a noun, usually by adding a suffix. "Hearing" comes from the verb "hear"; "appearance" from "appear," "recollection" from "recollect" and so on. The change is not just a matter of shifting from one word class to another: these single words can replace whole clauses. "The identification of" could otherwise read: "When X identified..," or "The fact that X identified...," or "To identify..." In terms of processing time, this is one instance in which shorter is not better.

g. *Passives.* Not all passives are hard to process, but when they turn up in subordinate clauses (e.g., "Most jury instructions are made even more incomprehensible than usual *when heard rather than read*"), they are difficult even for adults (Charrow & Charrow, 1979). Three-year olds tend to ignore passives in favor of word order, interpreting a question like "Were you chased by him?" as "Did you chase him?" (Fraser, Bellugi, & Brown, 1963; Reich, 1985). And while 4- and 5-year olds might understand that question in an adult fashion because it contains an action verb, "chase," they still make mistakes with non-action passives, as in the verb "love": "Was he loved by his mother?" (Tager-Flusberg, 1993). Most studies agree that children do not really control the passive form until they are around 10-13, but some scholars put it even later, at young adulthood (Romaine,1984; Horgan, 1978).

6. Putting two or more questions into one.

Questions don't have to contain legalese to be confusing to children. Combining even simple questions can make comprehension more difficult, and render answers less reliable. In fact, one study of multi-part questions put to children (Walker & Hunt, 1998) found that over 60% of their responses could not be tied accurately to the "question." The following are examples of question types to be avoided, each taken from real trials from my archives:

a. "And you saw this knife for the first time when and where?"
b. "But do you recall going to the hospital and will you tell us why you went to the hospital?"
c. "Are you saying it happened because it did or because your momma told you to say that?"
d. "Do you recall the last time you saw the knife: was it yesterday or last week?"
e. "Did you ever tell somebody that when you were, when, this is a person that would babysit for you and that you were afraid of Ettie Sue that Ettie Sue had a stick and she was going to get you?"

Each of these questions (put to children ages 4, 5, and 6) is difficult for a number of reasons, but the main point here is that in order to answer a question properly, children need to be able to remember it from beginning to end. Even though, by court standards, all but the last question are short, each one requires applying the same operation to two different parts of the question, thus effectively doubling its length, increasing its complexity, and placing a strain on short term memory. The result, predictably, is a high percentage of responses that do not *answer* the question (A.Walker, 1993; Walker & Nguyen, 1996, citing Hunt, et al., 1995). Children under 12 are still busy acquiring most of the skills connected with processing complex sentences (deVilliers & deVilliers, 1978). It makes little sense to add memory overload to their tasks.

7. Asking restricted choice questions.

Restricted choice questions (also called forced choice questions), do just what the name implies: they restrict the options for a "correct" response by hooking two or more possible answers together with the word "or" ("Was it big or little?"). Older children and adults recognize that neither choice may be the accurate one, and may say so, or deny knowledge or memory of either or all options given. But younger children may be uncertain how to respond. First, restricted choice questions are similar in form to that of Yes/No questions. Second, the fact that they are being asked by adult authority figures may suggest that no other options are available. Third, the children may either not know the information requested, or be unsure of it, but because they have learned that questions require answers, feel pressure to respond.

As a result of this uncertainty, these questions pose a particular threat to the fact-finding process with young children. A bare "Yes" or "No" may not only hide what they know, but make them appear incompetent: "Did it happen before or after Christmas?" "Yes." (A. Walker, 1999: 5-year-old found incompetent to testify by judge.) As that example suggests, younger children (preschool and kindergarten) have the most trouble responding accurately to these "or" questions, although experimental data suggests that if one of two options *is* correct, children from pre-school on are capable of choosing it whether it is in first or second position (N. Walker, 1997). All of the children in the Walker study had considerable difficulty, however, in providing their own answers if *neither* option was correct, or *both* options were correct, the preschoolers predictably being the most likely to make the mistake of choosing one of the two rather than supplying an answer of their own. In those cases, the option chosen was somewhat more likely to be the second than the first. No study was made of questions which contained more than two choices.

Clearly, restricted choice questions – which are direct rather than open-ended – create opportunities for error, particularly for children under eight or nine years old. But since direct questions are sometimes unavoidable in interviews with children whose narrative skills and cognitive development are not mature, one possible alternative is to give (no more than) three options, the last one always being open-ended, with each option presented in a fully formed question of its own: "Was it red, or was it blue – or was it some other color?" While there are no guarantees that such a technique will succeed, it at least provides an opportunity for a child to *supply* information rather than being restricted to options presented by a questioner.

8. Asking DUR/X (Do you Remember) questions (A. Walker, 1993).
One kind of complex Yes/No question that is particularly problematic in child interviews typically begins with a phrase like "Do you recall/remember" (DUR) followed by at least one more proposition (X), as in question "d" in paragraph 6 above: "Do you recall the last time you saw the knife..." (A single-proposition question like "Do you remember me?" is not a DUR/X question.) Interviewers of children should be concerned about questions like these because of the way that they are processed, and the answers that they generate.

When adults hear a question of this sort, they recognize from the opening phrase that they are expected to answer "Yes" or "No," and that the answer will be taken to mean that they affirm or deny however many propositions follow the word "remember." Responding appropriately to such a question entails being able to follow, process, and remember all of its parts. It also requires, especially if the question is a hostile one, being able to judge the intent of the questioner and make whatever modifications to the question that are necessary in order to answer truthfully. ("I remember 'a' and 'b,' of the question, but I'm not sure about 'c,' and I know that 'd' never happened.") *Children, even older school-age children, are not good at doing any of this.*

A particular problem with questions of this type is that adults seem to think that children *are* good at it, for they ask a lot of them, and act as if the Yes or No responses which they get are reliable indicators of a child's knowledge and/or belief. That can be a serious mistake, because while children may process these questions the same way adults do, they often do not, turning the answer into a response that has no validity (A. Walker, 1993).

A further problem with these questions is the ambiguity that often typifies them and their answers. Consider, for example, the following exchange between an adult and a 5-year-old girl:

Q. Do you remember telling T.J. that Harv pulled Doug's shirt up and dug at his eyes with a spoon?

A. No.

A logical adult interpretation of that response would be that the "No" meant that the child had no recollection of saying such a thing. And that is a possibility. But it could also have a number of alternative interpretations from the child's point of view: 1) that Harv did not pull up Doug's shirt; 2) that Harv did not dig at Doug's eyes with a spoon; 3) that it was not Harv but someone else who did one or both of those things; 4) that the child did not tell T.J. that, but told someone else. In fact, as further questioning revealed, her response meant none of these things. It simply meant, in her words, "I don't remember what you said." (A. Walker, 1993). Had the questioner not persisted in challenging the child's memory by asking follow-up questions, such an interpretation would never have been uncovered, and once again, a response that did not reflect the child's knowledge would have been taken to be a valid answer.

9. Asking questions that begin "I suggest to you that," "I submit to you," "I believe you told us," "Isn't it a fact that..." During cross-examination, attorneys are fond of asking questions in which they "suggest,"" believe," "submit" and otherwise cloak the statement that follows with language that asserts its status as fact. These questions serve as powerful tools of linguistic manipulation which even adults find difficult to counter, given the strikingly asymmetrical nature of the questioning process in court (A. Walker, 1987). *They are wholly inappropriate for children.* Young children already tend to believe that adults know everything, that adults are right about things (Walker & Warren, 1995), and that adults enter conversations *intending* to be clear, cooperative, and honest (Bonitatibus, Godshall, Kelley, Levering, & Lynch, 1988). When, therefore, an adult who is in a powerful position, in a forbidding, strange, and formal circumstance, "suggests" that something is a fact, it becomes extremely difficult if not impossible for children — even 11- and 12-year-olds — to know how to disagree if necessary, and to hold on, *verbally*, to what they know or believe to be true.

That is assuming, of course, that the question could be comprehended in the first place.

10. Asking children tag questions.
A tag question makes a statement and then adds a short question which invites corroboration of its truth (It's raining, *isn't it?* It isn't raining, *is it?*) and it is one of the most powerfully suggestive forms of speech that we have in the English

language (Danet, Hoffman, Kermish, Rafn, & Staymen, 1980; Woodbury, 1984). For that reason, and because in effect they allow the questioner to do the testifying, tag questions of all forms are the weapon of choice in cross examination (Morrill, 1976; A. Walker, 1987; Moore, Bergman, & Binder, 1996).

They are also surprisingly complicated linguistically. In order to answer a tag question of any kind correctly, the hearer must be able to carry out at least the following *seven* operations:

1. judge whether the statement part of the question (in the question above: "It is raining") is true or not;
2. translate the tag from its elliptical form to a full form (converting "is it" to "is it raining"; understand that the word "that" in the tag "isn't that true" is a substitute for the entire original question);
3. track what the pronouns in the question and in the tag refer to ("*That's one of the things* you told me about, isn't it? *She* looks nice, doesn't *she*?);
4. learn that a positive statement takes a negative tag ("It *is* raining, is*n't* it?") and vice versa ("It is*n't* raining, *is* it?"),
5. learn that the negative in a tag does not affect the main clause ("It is raining, is*n't* it/is it *not*?" does not mean that it is *not* raining);
6. understand that the tag expresses the point of view of the speaker, and does not necessarily mean that the statement is true;

   and finally,
7. learn how to meet or counter that point of view.

That is an extraordinarily complex operation, and it is no wonder that tag questions may not even show up in the speech of some children until the early teens (Dennis, et al., 1982, cited in Reich, 1986).

Three-and 4-year olds should not be expected to do *any* of the above (Brown, 1988). Five- and 6-year old English speakers from the mainstream American culture may understand only how they are *expected* to respond to simple tags like "is/isn't it?"; their responses may have nothing to do with whether they agree or disagree with the speaker. Children from cultures that treat negative questions in general differently from the way we do (e.g., Japanese) may not have even this basic knowledge. If the question is a long one, being able to hold in memory all the propositions in the question and check each one for truth before responding to a tag like "isn't *that* true?" (a "truth tag" question: A. Walker, 1987) is probably beyond the capability of any preteen.

It might be noted here, too, that questions that ask "Isn't it a fact... "(a form I identify as a pre-posed tag), or that use the "...isn't that a fact" tag require a child to know what a "fact" is.

Answers to truth tag questions tend, in any case, to be ambiguous: e.g., "Now, you testified earlier that Uncle C said he was going to kill you; is that right?" A "Yes" answer to that question could mean any one or more of the following: It is right that:

1. the child said she had "testified" something before (if she knows what "testify" means);
2. that it was Uncle C who said something;
3. that what Uncle C said was that he was going to kill her;
4. that all of it is correct.

Without clarification, it is impossible to know which possibility the child has in mind.

And finally, being able to resist both the psychological and linguistic pressure which a tag question exerts, in an atmosphere of distinctly asymmetric power, calls for a level of discourse sophistication that many adults never reach. *Tag questions of all kinds should be avoided with children.*

11. Shifting topics suddenly, particularly if it's a shift between the here-and-now, and the there-and-then.
Topic shifting is another one of those techniques of linguistic manipulation that is often used to keep adult witnesses off balance (A. Walker, 1987). But it is another technique that is inappropriate with children, not just when it is deliberate, as it may be during cross examination, but when it happens during the course of any kind of questioning. Because of children's naive status as discourse processors, and because young children live in the here-and-now, it makes sense – if the object is to get information and not to confuse – to give them clear and explicit clues that the subject is about to be changed: "Now, [child's name], I want to talk to you about X."; "All right. We just talked about X. Now I want to ask you about something different." (See Principle 11 on Framing.)

It also makes sense to avoid unnecessary and/or multiple shifts between the past and present within one question. The question put to a 5-year-old in a murder trial, "Do you remember [present] Martha asking you [past] 'Do you know who Mark is?' [present]"? makes two shifts; although it aims at knowledge of the past, it begins and ends in the present. A "Yes" response to that question is ambiguous ("Yes, I remember...," or "Yes, I know who Mark is"). "Did Martha ask you [past] who Mark is [present]?" gets at the same knowledge in a simpler way, and the response is less likely to be ambiguous. The question posed to a 4-year-old in a sex abuse trial, "Did anything happen to your dinky on this day?" mixed a past tense [did happen] with a demonstrative pronoun [this] which is more properly used to refer to the here-and-now than to the there-and-then. The child's "No" response, then, might have had nothing to do with a past event, but simply have been his denial that anything had happened to his dinky *on the day the question was being posed.*

12. *Asking children about relative concepts such as age, dimension, number, time, and kinship.*

It is almost impossible to envision an evidentiary interview with a child that does not include questions about how old, how big, how many, how long, when, and familial relationships. All of these questions deal with concepts, some of them more complex than others. As adults, we are used to hearing children talk about these things in our everyday lives. They

use terms like "old," "short," "ten minutes," "a hundred," "yesterday," "Aunt Mary," and so on, and they use them grammatically *in sentences*. However, most adults realize that children's use of these words does not necessarily imply that the children understand the concepts behind them.

Something seems to happen to that realization, however, when adults leave the everyday world and enter the world of law. They ask children questions such as "Is she older than me?" "Is he as tall as I am?" "How long did he leave his thing in your mouth?" "You say it happened yesterday?" "Is that your gramma on your mother's side or on your father's?" And then they apply the same standards to the children's responses that they do to those from adults. But that can be a critical error, as the following discussion – which departs from a strictly linguistic focus – demonstrates.

a *Age.* For young children, age is connected to size, and in particular, to height. "Tall" and "old" are directly related in their minds (Wood, 1981, citing Kuczaj & Lederberg, 1977). Given two people, one older but short, one younger but tall, children under the age of about 8 tend to pick the taller one as being older (Wood, 1981). If it is necessary to ask for judgments about age, then, it is a good idea to follow up on a child's answer to a question like "How old do you think he/she is?" by asking for some details. "What made you think she was old?" is a question some interviewers have found useful in this situation.

b. *Dimensions*. According to the partial-meaning theory of language acquisition, children learn the meaning of words in pieces, (deVilliers & deVilliers, 1978). The word "big" for instance, is generally thought to be encoded first as describing some positive pole of a physical dimension. But the words "tall," "wide," and "long" also belong to the same positive pole, and any one of them could contrast with "small," "short," or "little" (the negative poles). At least two other factors add to the confusion in children's use and understanding of words like these. One factor is a rigid application of these words. Children may know, for instance, that "tall" can apply to people, but not to buildings; "deep" may apply to a swimming pool, but not to a hole in the ground (deVilliers & deVilliers, 1978). A second factor is that from a perceptual viewpoint, as any adult knows, what is short to a grownup can be tall to a child. Either one of these factors can lead to mutual misunderstanding between adults and children. This is especially true with children between the ages of 2 and 6. Even with older children, however, it's wise for adults to be cautious in assuming that their meaning for these dimensional terms and the children's meaning are the same.

c. *Kinship*. Just as is the case with dimensional words, terms that express kinship are acquired feature by feature – a process that can continue until well into the teen years (Wood, 1981). Unlike most dimensional words, however, kinship terms vary considerably in their complexity. "Mother" and "father" differ in their relationship to a person only in one way – gender – and the terms are non-reciprocal: two people cannot be each other's mothers. "Sister" and "brother" also vary only by gender, but they are reciprocal and can apply to more than one other person. "Second cousin once removed" is

a term most adults would need paper and pencil to figure out, and even "grandmother" can be complicated to
a young child, for whom the notion of a parent *really*
having a parent is unfathomable. The more complex the
term, and the less exposure children have to people who
fit its description, the more difficult it is to acquire. Even
nuclear terms like "parent" can present problems to
9-year-olds (Chambers & Tavuchis, 1975), who can make
the error of equating "parent" with "adult," without realizing that to be a parent, one must have a child.
Children of blended and divided families may have special problems along this line. Another early error typical
of children is to associate a kinship term with a name
(e.g., "Uncle" is Uncle John's first name) (Reich, 1986)
and with age: thus, to them, only children – not adults –
can be brothers and sisters, and parents automatically
become grandparents when they get old.

A further complication in questioning children about
kinship is the fact that different cultures use kinship
terms in different ways. In most Native American tribes,
for instance, "mother" is any female in the community
who takes care of the child, and one child can have several mothers as well as having many parents (Cross,
1992). The same extension of word meaning is true of
many social groups in the United States, who have
adopted the terms "sister," "brother," and "cousin" for
non-familial relationships. "Father" is a term applied to
priests, and "aunts" and "uncles" may not be relatives at
all. Such apparent indiscriminate application of these
words, added to their underlying semantic complexity,
puts comprehension of the relations they express out of
the reach of children who are much under 10 years old.
The responsibility for discovering what the child's
meaning for these terms is, then, belongs to the questioner. See Chapter V, Section 1 for other important
cross-cultural kinship variables.

d. *Number*. The ability to count is often taken by adults to indicate a corresponding understanding of number concept. ("You counted for me, so you know about numbers. So how many times did he do this to you?": Walker & Warren, 1995). Children become proficient at counting somewhere between the ages of 2 and 5, and by 3 to 4 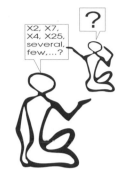 years of age, can determine that a group of three objects is bigger than a group of two. But when the groups being compared contain four or more items, children that young are likely to fail. Given two rows of six objects, one arranged to look longer than the other, children up to age 7 usually judge that the longer row has more objects in it. Even when children are able to solve problems of this sort, understanding the *concept* of number still may not be complete (Siegler, 1991). In any case, there is a very tenuous relationship between knowing how to count, knowing that six is bigger than three, or being able to pick four pencils out of a row of ten, and making an accurate assessment of how many times something happened. Not even adults can do that reliably.

It should be noted here, too, that there is a certain liability associated with asking the "How many times" question (Donna A. Rosenberg, personal communication). Because that question can be difficult even for adults to answer, and is age-inappropriate for young children, a response may change each time the question is posed, and/or be so wildly improbable (5-year-old: "10,000 times") or unsubstantiated as to raise serious doubts about a child's credibility. (One expert in interviewing reports that when she was a child she recalls telling her priest that she had "lied and disobeyed her mother 300 - 400 times a week." She was not aware of the exaggeration as either a lie or a misrepresentation. To her, knowing such "large numbers" was a source of

pride, and, as she reported, "would cover her bases.":
Poole & Lamb, 1998, p. 161, n.1). Interviewers, lawyers,
judges, juries – and parents – should keep in mind, then,
that unbelievable responses to this question can either be
a *metaphor* for "lots and lots of times," or simply a recognition that a question that has a number slot in it needs a
number to fill it.

e. *Time*. Time is another one of those concepts about which
children talk freely, in grammatical and appropriate
ways. But, once again, their use of words that express
clock, calendar, and durative time should not be taken as
an indicator that they can reliably give adults information about when or how long ago something happened,
or for how long it lasted. Neither should an inability to
name a date be taken as evidence that an event did not
happen.

Although estimates vary as to just when the time concept is fully mastered (Friedman, 1982), it is generally ac-
cepted that children begin to *tell* time at about age 7, but
how they learned to tell time should be investigated. It
may obscure a child's knowledge, for example, to ask
what the time is on a traditional wall clock if he learned
clock time by looking at a microwave. In general, the
safest approach to questions on time-related subjects is
probably the conservative one: not to expect
adult-satisfactory responses until children reach their
mid-teens (Friedman, 1982). In the mouths of
pre-adolescent children, phrases like "two months ago,"
"three hours," "it happened Friday," "in the spring,","a
long time ago" should not be taken literally, without further probing. It is probably better to phrase "When"
questions in particular, in terms of some familiar knowledge or concrete event in children's lives, such as break-
fast time, if school was out, what was on T.V., where it
happened, what the child had on, where mom was, and
so on. Even very young children can tie events to those
kinds of familiar temporal signposts.

In fact, that approach – taking the familiar, concrete path to get at children's knowledge, giving children a chance to choose among or provide their own examples, and avoiding all questions that are phrased abstractly ("What is truth?" "How well do you get along with your family?") – is a good one to adopt at all times when a child is on the receiving end of an adult's question.

13. Asking children, Do you know the difference between the truth and a lie?
It seems pretty plain from the studies that even at the age of 2-and-a-half, children possess the rudiments of knowing what it means to deceive (Chandler, Fritz, & Hala, 1989), and that by the age of 4, lies are understood as having two common components: 1) non-fact (Wimmer, Gruber, & Perner, 1984), and 2) something bad that you can get punished for (Piaget, 1932). It gets a bit more complicated than that: some children, for instance, believe that swearing is a lie; children as old as 11 can mix up what is a lie and what is a mistake (Piaget, 1932/1965). But essentially, and crucially for court purposes, factuality is what distinguishes truth from lies for young children (Burton & Strichartz, 1992). If it matches the facts, it's true; if it doesn't, it's a lie. Getting children to articulate that belief, however, can be a real problem.

The solution, however, does not lie in asking children, "Do you know the difference between the truth and a lie?" Not only does that question have little predictive value as to whether or not a child will report an event accurately (Goodman, et al., 1987; Saywitz & Lyon, 1997), it is, in essence, a waste of breath, because no matter what the response is, it cannot lead to a reliable decision as to competency. A "No" answer may lead to a false determination that the child is not competent to testify, when it more likely reflects a lack of ability to explain in words a very abstract concept. A "Yes"

answer requires a follow-on invitation either to define truth
("What is truth?") or to explain the difference ("What is the
difference?"). Each of these questions requires a child 1) to
know what it means for one thing to be different from another;
2) to have the cognitive capacity to compare, contrast, and abstract differences; and finally; 3) to apply linguistic skill to articulate those capacities_in the form of acceptable definitions or
explanations. That is an unrealistic task to set for a young
child.

Just how unrealistic has been impressively demonstrated by
the first empirical studies of young children's responses to typical competency questions (Lyon & Saywitz, 1999). The
4-to-7-year-old children tested were from multi-ethnic groups
who were involved in dependency court proceedings as a result of abuse and/or neglect. The studies showed *conclusively*
that *asking for a definition ("What is truth/a lie?") or explanation
of the difference* (the harder of the two tasks) *failed to demonstrate
the real competence of young children.* Asking children to *identify*
statements as true or false through use of hypothetical questions ("If I tell you X,..."), however, allowed almost all of the
5-year-olds to demonstrate credibly their understanding of
truth and lies. Even the 4-year-olds – who had difficulty in
making the distinction between "different" and "same" for
concrete objects – did better than chance with identification
questions. Because they seemed reluctant, however, to call a
statement made by the researcher a lie, Lyon and Saywitz cre-
ated a series of drawings in which two "generic" children
make true and false statements about objects.   The 4-year-olds'
task now was more concrete: they had only to point to the
child in the drawing who was telling the truth or a lie. Once
the "blame" factor was eliminated by having the lie, if there
was one, told by neither the adult questioner nor the child, the
4-year-olds no longer found it harder to identify a statement as
a lie than they did to identify a statement as true.

The degree of truth/lie competence demonstrated by these maltreated children from the dependency courts was particularly notable, since *all* of the maltreated children *fell 12-18 months below the normal curve* for both receptive and expressive language skills. Thus, the 4-year-olds were functioning at or below the level of non-abused 3-year-old children. Given the fact that the *5-year-olds* in this group demonstrated an impressive grasp of truth and lies, the researchers concluded that children even younger than 5 could be expected to qualify as competent, despite the stressful environment of court. Demonstrating that competence presumes, of course, age-appropriate questioning.

The ultimate purpose of the truth-qualification process is to establish that children have an appreciation for telling only what really happened. The Lyon and Saywitz studies strongly suggest that such a purpose can best be accomplished by first asking young children age-appropriate hypothetical questions which put the truth or lie in someone else's mouth. A series of short hypotheticals (e.g., "What if [a sibling] ate all mom's cookies? And what if he/she said you ate the cookies? Is [ ] telling the truth/lie?") can get at competence in ways that questions requiring definitions or explanations never could. Children 10 and older might be asked to give an example of a lie, and then tell why it is a lie, and what the truth would be. Appendix D offers some suggestions for the entire competency process.

Three final notes. One, "truth" and "lie" are vocabulary words. Vocabulary words are subject to interpretation by their users, and if children do not hear them used in the sense of "telling what really happened," or "intending to deceive," it is unlikely that you and they will be talking about the same thing. Vocabulary words also vary by region. In some parts of this country, "lies" are spoken of as "stories." Two, children may pick up the words "truth" and "lie" as part of a phrase that has more to do with emphasis than reality. "And that's the solemn truth," and "I tell you no lie" are not parsed for meaning by children, word for word. They simply serve a conversational purpose.

And finally, we adults *preach* "truth," but in everyday life, we often *teach* "lie." The phone rings, and we say, "Tell them I'm not here." We compliment someone, and later the child hears us make a derogatory remark about that same person. Given such behavior of adults, coupled with the complexity of the concepts, it is remarkable that young children grasp the essence of lies and truth at all.

14. Asking children if they understand you.

Adults should tell children at the beginning of every interview that if they don't understand a question, they should say so. There is a problem with that, however, in that children often will not comply. Young children sometimes mistakenly think that they do understand, (Walker & Warren, 1995) and children of all ages – like adults — are less likely to admit that they don't understand a question if they think that they should understand it, particularly if the atmosphere is forbidding and formal, as courts and other forensic environments are apt to be.

It becomes even more important, then, for adults to check regularly with children to see if they are in fact understanding the language they are hearing. Asking, "Do you understand?", however, is not the best way to find that out. If the answer is "Yes," the temptation is to accept that answer as true, and to move on. But that can be a mistake for the reasons mentioned above and in Principle 10. With preschool children, it might be better not to ask the question at all, but to check directly on the child's understanding. One way to do that might be to say, "I want to be sure I said that question the right way. So what do you think I asked you?" Or, "There was a hard word in that question. What do you think [X] means?" or even, "I wasn't listening very well. What did X just say/ask you?" A rote repetition by a child of the question or statement, however, is no guarantee of understanding, so following up with a question such as, "Can you say that in different words?" might help to uncover miscommunication between adult and child. Even when the question "Do you understand?" is used – as it can be with older children – it makes sense to follow up on "Yes" answers to be sure that the original question is the one that is going to be answered, and not the child's misinterpretation of it.

15. *Asking why questions.*

There are at least two kinds of why questions: objective ones ("Why is the sky blue?") and subjective ones ("Why did you say that the sky is blue?"). The second kind of question is common in examinations of child witnesses ("But do you recall going to the hospital and will you tell us why you went to the hospital?": question 'b' in Chapter III, Section 6 above). This kind of question presents children with two problems that make answering difficult. First, "Why ... you" questions in English are often perceived as critical or accusatory. Children in particular seem to regard them as requiring them to justify their actions rather than to describe what led up to a particular act (Boggs & Eyberg, 1990). Being on the defensive is not conducive to answering a question fully or accurately.

Second, answering even simple subjective "Why" questions (e.g., "Why did you wait so long to tell anybody?") requires the following metacognitive, cognitive and linguistic operations: 1) self-reflection, 2) reasoning from effect back to cause, 3) understanding that one has motivations, 4) figuring out what those motivations were at the time, 5) recapturing reasoning that may have taken into account possible consequences of the act and its effect on someone else, and 6) putting all that awareness into language that represents fully the reasoning behind the answer. Children are rarely prepared to meet this kind of challenge before they are at least 7 to 10 years old (Perry & Teply, 1985). The ability to respond reliably to questions that ask for inferences about the internal processes of behavior of others is not well established until children are 10 to 13 years old (Collins, Wellman, Keniston, & Westby, 1978). Even then – as with adults – the inferences may well be wrong.

16. Asking young children "How" questions.
Some "How" questions are easy for even very young children to answer appropriately. "How old are you?" and "How are you?" require only a memorized response ("Five"; "Fine"). But most "How" questions in interviews with children ask for more than memorization. Some require mastery of concepts (e.g., "How long did it last?", "How is she related to you?", "How often/ how many times..."), and the ability to reason from effect back to cause (e.g., "How come you did that?"). Others require not just narrative skills, but the ability to introspect, recognize intention, and flow of events: "How did that happen/come about?" All of those questions can be difficult even for older children (and some adults); they are problematic, if not impossible, for children ages 4-6, and are beyond impossible for the 2-3-year-old child. One expert in interviewing very young children has found that questions which seem on the surface very simple (e.g., "How did he do that?", asking for a verbal sketch of an act) get no useful responses at all (Sandra K. Hewitt, personal communication March, 1999). A shift from the abstract "how" to a concrete, action-oriented "Show me what he did," (when appropriate) is far more successful.

"How" questions, like "Why" questions, should be handled with care with children of any age. And except for the formulaic questions we teach even our youngest children ("How do you do?","How are you?","How old are you?"), they should be avoided when it is necessary to interview children under four.

17. Expecting children to give complete answers to non-specific questions such as, "Did anything happen?" or "What happened?"
These are some of the factors that make it hard for children to respond completely, (or in some cases, at all) to non-specific questions:

a. Dependence on the background knowledge of the questioner. Children give their first narratives to people who know a lot about them. Building a narrative is a cooperative venture, with the adult asking specific questions ("He hit you? Who hit you? Where were you? What were you doing? Did you hit him back?") to fill in the details children do not supply on their own. In the absence of questions of that sort, young children are left without a means of knowing what is important to tell, and in what order to tell it.

b. Incompletely developed story model. (See Principle 14). Story models – also known as story grammars (Stein & Glenn, 1979) – organize all the What, Who, Where, When, How, and Why's that adults are interested in when they ask a child, "What happened?" Story models are what make it possible to tell a narrative in the absence of outside questioning, and until they are fully developed, children's narrative responses to non-specific questions are likely to be incomplete.

c. Inability to narrow the field on their own. Adults would have the same problem if they were led to a window, shown a scene outside and asked, "What's there?" Knowing how to answer would depend on knowing what was important to tell, which in turn would depend on understanding the context of the question and the needs of the hearer. Adults in that situation would know the right questions to ask to narrow the field if they could not do so by themselves. Children generally do not.

d. A difference in the child's focus. Questions about what happened are not the same in court as they are at home. In court, they call not for a fresh or spontaneous telling, but for a *re*telling of a specific event that adults want to hear about. In spontaneous reports, the child is already focused on the event. In retellings, the child may be unfocused until given a specific prompt by someone else.

Consider the following exchange in a sex abuse case between a 7-year-old child and her attorney:

Q. Can you tell me what he did the other time?
A. He pulled me inside my house, and then, and then I fell asleep on the couch.
Q. What happened?
A. [Silence]
Q. M, did something happen?
A. No.

For the child, that was true: her story was over ("I fell asleep on the couch") and there was nothing more to tell. But her story also was incomplete, and the attorney's "What happened," and "Did something happen," were intended to redirect her focus to *what happened in the middle.* Those questions, however, assumed an adult's ability to understand his intention. Unfortunately, her questioner did not recognize that the child's interpretation and his intention did not match, and because both of the timing of his first question, and its lack of specificity, she was unable to give him the information he needed. As a result, the child's response was interpreted as a denial that any abuse had occurred on that occasion; her report remained incomplete, and all the details in the middle that the court was there to hear about remained unheard (Walker & Warren, 1995).

18. Asking questions that require tracking who said what to whom when.

Cross examination generates many questions that ask children to compare what they have said or been told on one occasion with what they have said or been told on another. Unavoidably, those questions are multi-layered. That not only makes them difficult to comprehend, but requires that 1) children retrieve from memory what actually was said, 2) keep track of the truth value of each part of the question, 3) analyze words, phrases and syntax the way adults can (Garbarino, Stoot, et al., 1992), – and then 4) answer in an unambiguous way. It is a particularly difficult task if the questions were about things that were irrelevant or uninteresting to the child, such as the color of an object or details about a room in which a crime occurred (Davies & Seymour, 1997) and/or the original conversation was not understood. One cannot remember accurately, if at all, what cannot be understood (Charrow & Charrow, 1979.)

While older children may be able to accomplish all of these tasks, or ask for clarification if they cannot, it is completely unreasonable to expect such skill in a 4-year-old (or even older children) when confronted with a not-untypical question like this one from a custody hearing: "And did your mommy tell you that if you were asked if mommy had told you to say that daddy peed in your mouth that you were to say it really happened?" Despite the understandable desire of questioners to know the conversational history of a child's answers, that type of question is simply futile. It is incomprehensible. There are some kinds of questions that should never be put to children, and questions that ask children to track who said what to whom and when is one of them.

19. Asking "jello" questions.

Take jello into your hand, squeeze it, and it squirts away. It has no real boundaries, and is impossible to grasp. Like jello, questions that are vaguely worded, that use abstract words instead of concrete ones, or for that matter, that ask about abstract concepts, can elude children's understanding. Phrases like "area behind the house," "was there screaming," "did your pants ever come off," "what is it to tell the truth?" require solidification in order to be clearly understood. "In the back yard," "Did you hear a scream?" substitute concreteness for the abstract. Pants don't normally "come off" by themselves; someone takes them off. And because "truth" is an abstract concept in itself (see Section 13 above) questions that ask for an articulation rather than demonstration of knowledge of truth are unlikely to elicit useful answers, particularly when they use an open-ended form (What is it...) that provides no boundaries, no mold, to guide an answer. Better results can be achieved with children if the questions they are asked use concrete (simple, familiar) nouns and verbs, acts are given agents, and abstractions of all kinds are avoided.

IV. Things to look out for in children's answers

1. Idiosyncratic use of words.

When children don't have a word to fit an experience, they make do with one they already have. Thus, in many cases of sexual abuse, children have reported being stabbed, despite the absence of a knife or injury. But to them, "stab" apparently describes what the experience *fell like*. Children also reinterpret words they hear to fit ones they know: "veterinarian," for example, was used by a 10-year-old to describe someone who had served in the Armed Forces. A "jury" could be a trip for one child, or "that stuff you wear on your neck and finger like a ring" for another (Saywitz, 1989). Early learners of language overgeneralize: "Daddy" may be any tall man in uniform who comes to the front door; on the other hand, they can undergeneralize: "kitty" may be used by a child to fit only the family pet. By analogy, children create new words based on what they know about the world: a small caterpillar becomes a "kittenpillar"; a butterfly is (much more logically) a "flutter-by." New words are usually easy to recognize for what they are, but words that are familiar to adults may pass by unnoticed, and lead to an incorrect interpretation of what the child has said.

2. Children's use of pronouns.

It is easy to recognize the error when a 3-year-old says, "Her came home," but not so easy to know that a child of tender years can talk about "my book" and mean "your book" (Charney, 1980). As late as 8 years old, children can begin sentences with a pronoun that does not refer to the most recently mentioned person (Amye Warren, personal communication). Hearing the following report, for example, "I saw John and Mac come in. He had a big knife," most adults would probably put the knife in Mac's hand. But for children still in this stage, the knife could well be held by John.

Even when children have mastered personal pronouns, however, they can do to adults the same thing that adults often do to them and to each other: use "he" or "she" or "we" to refer to people whose identity they know, but the hearer may not. *Pronouns are dangerous words*, as are all indexicals (see Chapter III, Section 2). It is very important, if clear communication is the goal, that adults make sure they know what these words mean when children use them. It is equally important to give children immediate or very recent referents for the pronouns adults themselves use. In fact, a good rule to follow is, "The fewer the pronouns the better."

3. Responses to the following kinds of Yes/No questions. Questions that:

1. contain more than one idea,
2. are preceded by "Do you remember/recall," and/or
3. have a truth tag like, "is that true/right/so."
4. take the form of "Did you not..."

Both "Yes "and "No" responses to any of those questions can be ambiguous – a fact which should be of some interest to any forensic interviewer, given that Yes/No questions outnumber other kinds of questions put to children in studies of both court proceedings and Child Protective Service interviews by as much as 4 to 1 (A. Walker, 1987; Warren & McGough, 1996). See Chapter III, Sections 7 and 8 for further discussion.

That fact in itself is cause for concern for at least two reasons. First, by definition, Yes/No questions leave no room for information to come from the hearer: they expect only a "Yes" or a "No" in response. Second, interviewers rarely follow up on a "Yes" or "No" answer to see if either one really means what we adults would take it to mean. Given the kind of questions listed above, that failure can result in responses from children that do not reflect what they really know: a situation that can put the truth-finding process in considerable jeopardy.

4. *"I don't know"responses.*

"I don't know" is a response that some people use when they have absolutely no idea what the answer is, and others use to express uncertainty even when they are almost sure of their knowledge.

According to one study (Linn, 1987, cited in Brennan & Brennan, 1988), people who are unwilling to take risks in answering questions use "I don't know" more often than risk takers do. The study also noted a gender difference: females in the study were more likely to use "I don't know" than males. Considering the high stress associated with answering questions both before and during trial, it would not be surprising to discover that the use of "I don't know" by children both young and old could be attributed to a reluctance to take a risk, rather than to a lack of knowledge.

There is also the possibility that given the stressful environment of the court, "I don't know" can indicate a simple unwillingness to answer the question (Perry, Kern, Eitemiller, Mohn, Fischer, & Stessman, n.d.), or an inability to do so, particularly if the child feels intimidated by the questioning situation (Saywitz & Nathanson, 1993).

5. *Answers that merely repeat what the child has said before.*

Even before they are 2 years old, children can interpret a "What?" to mean that they have not been understood, and can modify a simple two or three word sentence ("It ball/it big ball") to try to make a statement clearer (Gallagher, 1977). But generally, children under about 9 or 10 do not have the linguistic skills to vary their messages significantly, so they sometimes just repeat what they have said before. They might realize that they are not being understood, but be unable to do anything about it, in which case it is not stubbornness, or lack of intelligence, or unwillingness to cooperate that generates these answers.

V. Some additional considerations in communicating with children

1. *Cultural differences.*

A loose definition of culture might be: "All those things – attitudes, beliefs, values, practices – that we need to know to oper-
ate successfully in a society." Like language, culture not only
binds a group of people together, it separates them from others, creating a filter that lets certain information in, keeps other
information out, and reinterprets information according to our
cultural beliefs and expectations. When that filter operates
unconsciously – when it is unrecognized – the result can be
misinterpretations which, in the legal arena, can be crucial.

It is essential to realize that *no culture is homogeneous.* As of
the 1990 census, for instance, the term "Native American," included 542 tribes, each with its own idiosyncrasies; each having members who assimilate in varying degrees to the
"American" ways. Every culture, however, has a set of criteria
for determining the truth of a statement, and those criteria cut
across almost every aspect of communication, both content and
delivery. Principle 17 touched on a number of them without ty-
ing the criteria to a particular culture. What follows are a few
additional culture-specific linguistic elements that can have an
important effect on children's responses to our questions, and
on our related judgments of the children's competence and
credibility.

Pausing. For Native Americans, silence is an integral part of
communication. Their long pauses between phrases, sentences, and after questions tend either to be interpreted neg-
atively in our mainstream culture, or result in lost
information when a new question comes too quickly. Such

use of silence contrasts markedly with the style of native Hawaiian children (Berk, 1997, citing Tharp, 1989, 1994; Watson-Gegeo & Boggs, 1977), and many African American (Abney, 1999) and Jewish children whose elders treat rapid-style, overlapping speech not as rude interruptions, but as welcome and expected involvement with the other speaker(s) (Tannen, 1985).

Kinship terms. In many cultures, kinship terms can refer to someone other than a relative. "Uncle" in Laotian, Japanese, and most Indian tribes, for instance, can refer to a friendly older male, an older man, or a friendly younger male, respectively. "Grandfather/mother" are terms of respect in Japanese for any much older man and woman; for Laotians and Native Americans, "grandfather" can mean a friendly older male. Kinship terms in general are difficult for children to master; they can be even harder – and much more consequential – for adults to sort out when children from our own social groups, much less those from other cultures, use them. See also Chapter III, Section 12e.

Time. In mainstream America, time rules. We run our lives by the clock, and give names to each segment of its passage. But time flows more slowly in Hispanic and Arabic cultures; Native Americans mark life events not by measurable segments but by seasons, ceremonies, and daily activities. The different values placed on time by these cultures can make tardiness seem like rudeness, and can increase the difficulty young children already have in responding to questions that ask "how many times" or "when." Chapter III, Section 12e gives further non-culture specific details on this difficult concept.

Self-effacement. In contrast to the value put on assertiveness in mainstream American culture, harmony and self-effacement are two important values for both Asians (Chan, 1992;

Okamura, Heras, & Wong-Kerberg, 1995), and Native Americans (Joe & Malach, 1992). These values can be expressed in a variety of linguistic ways which can obscure credibility: seeming to agree in order not to offend, choosing not to defend oneself in deference to an authority, smiling to cover embarrassment or shame, or qualifying all statements of knowledge (Morrow, 1992). Children from cultures that place high value on unquestioning loyalty to and respect for elders – Hispanic, African American, Asian, and Native American to name a few (Lynch & Hanson, 1992) – have an even higher bar than most to overcome when they are asked to discuss sensitive, family-related subjects with yet another authority figure who is a stranger: the adult questioner. The fact that many of these children speak the language of their culture as their native tongue makes accurate communication that much more difficult, as discussed below in Section 2.

Color categories As a footnote to some of the more critical cultural "differences that make a difference" noted above, it might be worth commenting on the connection among culture, colors, and forensic questioning of children. As English-speakers, we take our color terms for granted, and use them in the majority of our hypothetical truth/lie questions ("If I said my shirt is green, ...") (Huffman, Warren, & Frazier, 1998; Walker & McKinley-Pace, n.d.). We ask color questions in our attempts to identify people, places, and things, and in research on children's suggestibility. We do it without realizing that color categories are culturally determined, and that the ability to discriminate between one color and another has a great deal to do with the connection between language and culture.

It is difficult to talk about, or even perceive, something for which you have no name, and colors are no exception. Black and white are universal in all languages, after which come red, then green and yellow (singly or together), blue, then brown, and finally pink, purple, orange and gray in no particular order (Berlin & Kay, 1969). Even then, distinctions among those colors are not always clear. The Japanese "aoi" includes blue, green, and the fact that something is pale. In some Native American languages, Zuni and Navaho for example, the difference between yellow, orange, and red is either non-existent or blurred (Bolinger & Sears, 1981, citing Landar, Ervin, & Horowitz, 1960). Since children learn the color categories of their native languages, and those categories shape their perceptions, using color as an identifier with a child for whom English is a second language can result in responses that seem inaccurate, contradictory, or just plain incompetent. The immediate remedy is simple, one that is recommended in Poole and Lamb (1998): ask the child to label the color of some object you are pointing to. But the broader remedy is more difficult. It requires that we recognize that culture is embedded in language, and stay alert to culture-based perceptions that might alter our opinions of the testimony of a child, whether the child is a non-native speaker of English, or simply from an ethnic group that is different from our own.

2. English as a Second Language (ESL).

Children from other cultures who speak English as a second language bear at least six additional burdens in forensic interviews and courtroom proceedings beyond that of simply being children. They are at greater risk because, first, deciphering what is heard in a second language is more difficult for anyone. Rapid speech rates, regional accents, and lack of familiarity with idioms, speaker intention, and the subtleties of the English language add to problems already posed by the fact that as children, they are still in a process of linguistic and cognitive growth.

Second, interference from one's own native language can cause adults as well as children to make errors in their speech which lead to an unintended meaning (Gumperz, 1982; Lund & Duchan, 1993). One critical interference error for speakers from Japan or Polynesia, for example, is in responding to Yes/No questions that begin with negative contractions. In

English, if the information in the question, *"Aren't* you Mary Jones?" is true, the answer is *"Yes* (I am)"; otherwise, the answer is "No (I am not)." But for Polynesians (Lane, 1984) and the Japanese, the responses are exactly opposite. "Yes," means "Yes, I am *not* (Mary Jones)"; *"No,"* means "No, I *am* (Mary Jones)."

Third, non-native speakers of English are strangers in the questioners' land, unfamiliar with the customs, culture, and language of the law, while, fourth, their questioners are on home ground, speaking in their mother tongue and operating from a position of power. Fifth, as of this writing, most of their questioners have had little education in conducting age-appropriate proceedings even in their own language.

And, critically, sixth, children's speech and behavior are judged not by their *own* language and cultural norms, but by those of their listeners – interviewer, judge, jury (Lane, 1984). For those listeners, an intonation pattern learned by children whose parents come from India might be interpreted by native-English speakers as rude or disrespectful (Gumperz, 1977), and the soft, slow, pausing speech typical of many Native Americans, especially if accompanied by downcast eyes, might be heard as indicators of a lie. Misinterpretations such as these are not uncommon, even among adult speakers in everyday life. Their effect, however, is much more consequential in the legal world.

It would be impractical, if not impossible, for any of us to know all we need to know about how other language structures and cultural beliefs might affect our judgments of the children we see before us. But being willing to consider an interpretation other than the one imprinted on us by our own culture would be a step in the right direction.

VI. Why are there inconsistencies in children's testimony? A few language-related reasons.

1. *Children may be both speaking and responding to your questions in a literal way.* As referred to in Principle 6, this tendency is particularly true of young children, who can be remarkably sensitive to the words used in a question. Asked, "Are you in school?" a young child who at a later time described what she does in first grade responded, "No." To an adult, this was inconsistent; to the child it was perfectly logical: at the time of the question, she was in court, not in school, as anyone could plainly see. Subtle changes in the grammar of a repeated question can also elicit answers that appear to be inconsistent: "Were you hurt?" (an abstract phrasing) "No"; "Did you get hurt?" (a concrete phrasing) "Yes." Questioners of young children must keep in mind that children view the world and language through a lens that is much narrower than ours; failure to take that narrow view into account can have unfortunate consequences.

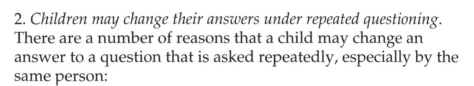

CATALYST

2. *Children may change their answers under repeated questioning.* There are a number of reasons that a child may change an answer to a question that is asked repeatedly, especially by the same person:

    a. As a general rule of conversation, the repetition of a question implies, even to adults, that the first answer was somehow unacceptable.

    b. In a related reason, children may know that their answer is correct, but may change it, not because of a lack of confidence in their own response, but because of incorrect perceptions about a questioner's intentions. That is, they may believe that the questioner already knows the answer to the question that is being repeated, and so regard the questioner as insincere (Perner, Leekam, & Wimmer, 1986).

c. Lack of experience with a task can lead to uncertainty and lack of confidence in one's own ability to answer correctly (Gelman, Meck, & Merkin, 1986). This is true of adults as well as of children.

d. The age of a child and type of question can make a difference. Older children are fairly consistent in the information they give in response to repeated open-ended questions or invitations (e.g., "Tell me about..."), whether the repetition is during one interview or across several (Memon & Vartoukian, 1996). Younger children's responses to repeated broad open-ended questions, however, while highly accurate (Fivush & Shukat, 1995), tend to yield different details about the same event.

e. The task may simply be unattractive, and children may figure that the best way to end it is just to change the answer to the one the adult seems to want (Siegal, 1991).

f. Children do not expect an adult questioner to try to trick them, so if a child's answer is, for example, repeated sarcastically, followed by a question like, "Is *that* what you were saying/Is *that* what you mean to tell me?" the child's belief that adults are right, and honest (see Chapter III, Section 9 above) may lead to a changed response.

g. The child may simply not have understood the first question.

3. *Different questions by different questioners in different surroundings may elicit different details.* Not even adults can guarantee that all of the details of a personally experienced event will spring to mind when they are first questioned about it, nor can they guarantee that some of the details will not change when

they have had more time to think about the event. And that is despite the fact that as adults, they have presumably internalized a mental structure called a story model or schema which serves both as an encoding and retrieval aid (see Principle 14). In young children, however, especially preschool children, this structure and other retrieval mechanisms are in rudimentary form, which makes children heavily dependent in giving their reports on questions that are asked of them by adults. And as a rule, they respond only to the question asked, instead of using it as a springboard to provide more details (Fivush, 1993). Therefore, if the questions differ in focus from occasion to occasion, the details can be expected to differ as well.

The relative complexity of questions during one interview as compared with another may also yield different responses. Children's attention tends to wander when the questions are too dense, too long, and too complicated for them to comprehend (and they are questioned for too long). Adults react no differently. The problem is compounded by the fact that children are much less likely than adults to ask for clarification. So if a question asked at one time was phrased simply, but at another time was too complex for a child to understand, the answers could very well change – and probably would.

The *attitude of a questioner* can also have an effect on how much information a child is able and willing to give. Studies have shown that an objective but benign attitude on the part of the interviewer facilitated accuracy (Carter, Bottoms, & Levine, 1996) and significantly increased the amount of information a child was able to give, while not increasing errors. A colder, distant attitude on the part of the interviewer actually increased the amount of inaccurate information given by preschoolers (Goodman & Clark-Stewart, 1991). It takes no great leap of imagination to conclude that a hostile, aggressive questioner can have a strongly negative effect on the ability of a child to recount details. It works that way with adults, as well. Thus, if a child is questioned about the same incident by two interviewers who have markedly different interviewing styles, some inconsistency in the details given by the child can be expected.

Speech styles – accent, rate of speech, intonation, pausing – can vary from questioner to questioner during trial or across interviews. Adult listeners often need time to adapt to a speaker's voice before being able to identify a word (Lieberman, 1963). Children can be expected to have more difficulty, particularly in a court environment when the language itself is strange.

And finally, variations in the physical environment of the interview can contribute to inconsistent testimony from a child. Studies have shown that both the quality and quantity of information a child is able to give are affected by the surroundings in which the questions are asked (Davies & Seymour, 1997; Saywitz, 1995). Given a familiar and informal environment, the statements children make about the events they have participated in are more complete than those given in formal and forbidding surroundings (Saywitz & Nathanson, 1993).

4. *When children have to talk about novel experiences*, they can misapply words that are only tentatively under their command. Terms like "before," "after," and "because" can be misused by preschool children who are trying to describe a sequential or causal relationship that they don't yet fully understand (French & Nelson, 1985). Relational terms can also be a source of apparent inconsistency when children use them accurately to describe familiar daily events ("I got up before Mom did"), but fail to understand them when used by someone else, particularly when it is an event with which they are not familiar ("Before the two cars crashed together, what were you and your mom talking about?").

5. *Incomplete acquisition of a linguistic rule, such as the before/after mentioned above, and all of the other words discussed in Chapter III,* can lead a questioner to believe that a child's answers are inconsistent with the truth. Pronouns can be particularly troublesome, aside from their characteristic ambiguity discussed in Chapter III, Section 2. Children under 5, for instance, are particularly prone to ignoring pronouns that look ahead, as does the "he" in the following question: "When he came in, did you tell your Dad what happened?" If a child does not hear the "he" and "dad" in that question as being connected, the answer might well be "Yes," but the meaning might be, "Yes, I told Dad" [at some unspecified time]. If later on, the child (truthfully) denies having told his/her father when he came in, the result is an apparent inconsistent statement.

6. *Children learn very early to be cooperative conversationalists* (Bloom, 1991). In our society, that cooperation includes knowing how to follow our "turn-taking" rules: I take a turn, you take a turn, I take a turn, you take a turn; *I ask you a question, you give me an answer.* And so, in an attempt to follow that cultural/conversational rule, children may stretch to provide answers to questions that they have not fully understood. The result of such ad hoc replies can easily be contradictory. Questions that use complicated verb forms, negation, age-inappropriate language, complex constructions, questions that call on children to perform metacognitive operations (such as thinking about thinking) that they are ill-equipped to carry out, are questions that are begging to be answered inconsistently.

7. *Adult assumptions about what children mean can create inconsistencies that don't exist.* Superordinate, or "higher order" words pose a particular problem. Adults know that "vehicle" includes under its umbrella several hyponyms such as "bus," "car," "van," "truck." "Animal" can include "pet," under which fall "dog," "cat"... "Residence" includes "house," "home," "apartment," "trailer," even "city," "town" – or more specifically, "Chicago." Not being able to recognize those

relationships can cast doubt on a child's credibility, as it did in the case of a child whose response during trial to the question, "What *city* did it [the abuse] happen in?" was "I don't know," when in a pre-trial interview, she had given a place name that she knew only as a *town*.

"Vehicle" and "residence" are adult words, but "clothes," "touch," and "move" discussed earlier, are not. Yet, as higher order words, they can create the appearance of inconsistency when child and adult are thinking on different planes. It's a question of the adult not understanding what the child means.

But adult assumptions about a *child's* ability to understand what the *adult* means can also be at fault. Adults rely on other adults to track topics of conversation, and to alert each other if a sudden change of topic has been confusing. They rely on each other to understand some of our shorthand ways of speaking: leaving out at the end of a statement, for example, a fact that is assumed to be known by the listener(s): "Well, it all happened on the same day [that I missed the train]." But as has already been pointed out, children can *not* be relied upon to know what is going on in adults' heads, and/or what adults mean. Children, especially the very young children, need to be kept on track, and need to have adults be explicit. *It does not pay to assume.*

8. *Failure to ask follow-up questions.* Getting accurate information from children is a task made difficult by legions of problems, among which are the developmental level of a child, the skill of the interviewer, the establishment of rapport, the specter of suggestive questioning, and the often inordinate delays between the time a child is questioned, and the time that the case is adjudicated. But added to that list is the tendency of adults to assume, once again, that they and the child are speaking the "same" language, so there is no need to follow up on responses as simple as "Yes," and "No."

Unquestioned responses, particularly when they concern a crucial facet of a case, can create unintended inconsistencies between the facts and a child's statement. "Black" to a young child describing a white man ("Was he a black man? "Yes") meant simply that his face and hands were covered with dirt. To another child, the response "Black" to the question, "What color was the car?" meant that it was nighttime, and very dark *inside* the car. Both inconsistencies between facts and answers could have been explained by the follow-up question, "What do you mean when you say [he/it] was black?"

Reducing "inconsistencies that are not" takes curiosity, imagination, a desire to uncover the truth, and a bridge between response and the next question. "What do you mean when you say..." is one bridge. "How did you figure that out?" is another. And, simply, "Tell me more about that" can get at the difference between what children *say* and the knowledge they have in their heads.

9. *Taking at face value children's responses to "concept" questions (those that ask about age, size, time, kinship, distance, repetition...)* This cause of inconsistency is related, of course, to the failure to ask follow-up questions. It is included here as a separate category because it is such a common and often critical error that can be avoided, as it was in the following example.

> "How long did you live there?" (to an 8-year-old).
> "Two months."
> "Did you live there when school started?"
> "Yes."
> "Well, then," (speaking in June) "that'd be about 9 months, I guess."

"Month" is so ordinary a word that we take for granted schoolchildren's understanding of what it signifies in terms of time. But while we can teach children "months" of the year as a list to be learned by rote – along with all our other cultural lists – we cannot teach them to understand the concept of time. That is a developmental process; and until the concept of time and the words that express time meet, we can have no assurance that "two months" means what we think it does. Fortunately for the credibility of the child above, her interviewer exercised the curiosity and imagination that is often required to discover the truth when we question children, and prevented what could later have been characterized as an inconsistent statement.

10. *Everything thus far discussed in this book has the potential to create an apparent inconsistent statement.* Any inaccurate or incomplete processing of a question or its intention, any adult ignorance of children's language and cognitive development, any clash of cultural backgrounds and norms, any misunderstanding between questioner and child can lead to an apparent inconsistency in a child's statements. It is possible, of course, for an inconsistency to be real: fact-based rather than interpretation-based. But in the forensic setting, the penalty for inconsistency is a heavy one: it casts a dark shadow over the credibility of any witness. Given the vulnerability of children as less experienced discourse processors than their questioners, it is all the more important that adults not let that shadow fall for the wrong reasons.

11. And finally, the reason that underlies all of the above: *children are not adults.* Their cognitive system, their linguistic system, their inter-relational and conversational abilities all are in a state of growth. While the information that adults seek may be firmly lodged in children's memories, children are still developing skills in retrieving it, packaging it, and reporting it in ways that adults can understand. The external forensic system in which children are expected to retrieve information is a system that was built *by* adults *for* adults. It is a system that uses often arcane language in an adult environment under adult rules which are frequently intimidating even for adults themselves. Under such circumstances, it is not surprising that some inconsistencies – both real and imagined – should occur in a child's testimony.

VII. Conclusion

In his book, Language of the Law, Mellinkoff (1963:vii) wrote: "With communication the object, the principle of simplicity would dictate that the language used by lawyers agree with the common speech, unless there are reasons for a difference."

Although his was a book written by a lawyer for lawyers, and the common speech to which he referred was the one that adults use with each other in daily life, his advice is still painfully relevant today to our communication with the children who come into our courts. If, in fact, communication is the object, then it just will not do for us to ignore the special principle of simplicity. It also will not do for us to just guess what "simple" for a child might be. We need some proven guidelines, and that is what this book has been meant to provide.

The people for whom it has been intended – the lawyers who pose the last evidentiary questions to children, and the judges who listen to those questions, and ask some of their own – are an extraordinarily crucial audience. The lawyers bear the final responsibility of enabling children to tell what they know; the judges act as the last gatekeepers for clear communication in their courts. If together they fail to understand that the standard of "common speech" among adults is not one that can be applied to children, then the result may well be not discovery of facts, but fostering of confusion which is then mistaken for fact.

There is a natural concern among the judiciary that the scales of justice not be unfairly tipped toward either accused or accuser. And some see any attempt at modifying the language of the courts, or the language of questioning as prejudicial to one side or the other. But learning to communicate accurately with children is not a matter of tipping the scales. It is a matter of reaching for equal access to understanding for *everyone* who enters the legal system: adult and child, plaintiff, defendant, and victim. It is hard to imagine how anyone's rights could be jeopardized, or how justice could be anything other than well served, if we apply to everyone, including children, the principle of simplicity in speech.

Appendix A: Checklist for Interviewing/Questioning Children

Developed by Anne Graffam Walker, Ph.D.
Revised February 1994

I. Framing the Event

1. Did I tell the child my name and what my job is—in non-technical words?
2. Did I help the child become familiar with the surroundings of the interview?
3. Did I tell the child the purpose of our talk, and why it is important, and what will happen afterward?
4. Did I give the child a chance to ask me questions about this talk? Did I try to establish a common vocabulary for the things we talk about? Was I listening to the kind of words and sentences that the child used?

II. Using Clear Language

5. Did I use easy words instead of hard ones? (Do I know what a "hard" word is?)
6. Did I avoid legal words and phrases?
7. Did I use words that mean one thing in everyday life, but another thing in law?
8. Did I assume that because a child uses a word, he or she understands the concept it represents?
9. Was I as redundant as possible? That is, did I use specific names and places instead of pronouns (like "he" and "she") and vague referents (like "there" and "that")?

III. Asking the Questions

10. Did I keep my questions and sentences simple? Did I try for one main (new) thought per utterance?

11. Did I avoid asking "DUR-X" questions? [Questions that begin, "Do you remember," followed by one or more full propositions.]

12. When I shifted topics, and when I moved from the present to the past or vice versa, did I alert the child that I was going to do so?

13. Did I give the child the necessary help in organizing his or her story?

14. Did I avoid asking the child about abstract concepts, like, "What is truth?" Did I choose instead to give the child everyday, concrete examples and let him or her *demonstrate*, rather than *articulate* knowledge of truth and lies, right and wrong?

15. Did I use as few negatives as possible in the questions I asked?

IV. Listening to the Answers

16. Were the child's *responses* to my questions, or *answers* to my questions? Am I sure?

17. If the child's answers were inconsistent, did I ask myself if:
   a. I had asked the exact same question repeatedly?
   b. I had changed the wording of a question I had asked before?
   c. I was forgetting that children can be very literal in their interpretation of language?
   d. The child's processing of language might not be as mature as mine?

V. Global Checks

18. Did I stay in the child's world by framing my questions in terms of the child's experience?

19. Did I take the child's understanding of language for granted?

20. Was I listening to my *own* language, my *own* questions?
21. Did I ask myself before I began: Am I gathering information, or am I doing therapy?

Appendix B: A Few Suggestions for Questioning Children

Developed by Anne Graffam Walker, Ph.D.
Revised March 1999

General precepts:

1. Reduce the processing load that children must carry: aim for simplicity and clarity in your questions. If the child uses simple words and short sentences, so should you.

2. Be alert for possible miscommunication. If a child's answer seems inconsistent with prior answers, or doesn't make sense to you, check out the possibility that there is some problem 1) with the way the question was phrased or ordered, 2) with a literal interpretation on the part of the child, or 3) with assumptions the question makes about the child's linguistic/cognitive development or knowledge of the adult world.

Some specifics:

1. Break long sentences/questions into shorter ones that have one main idea each.

2. Choose easy words over hard ones: use Anglo-Saxon expressions like "show," "tell me about," or "said" instead of the Latinate words "depict," "describe," or "indicated."

3. Avoid legal jargon, and "frozels" (my term for frozen legalisms) like "What if anything," "Did there come a time."

4. It is important that you and the children use words to mean the same thing, so run a check now and then on what a word means to each child. Although children generally are not good at definitions, you can still ask

something like, "Tell me what you think a ____ is," or "What do you do with a ___?" "What does a ___ do?" Don't expect an adult-like answer, however, even if the word is well-known. The inability to define, for example, "wind" does not mean that the person does not know what the wind is. Definitions require a *linguistic* skill.

5. Avoid asking children directly about abstract concepts like what constitutes truth or what the difference is between the truth and a lie. In seeking to judge a young (under 9 or 10) child's knowledge of truth and lies, ask simple, concrete questions that make use of a child's experience. Ex: I forgot: how old are you? (Pause) So if someone said you are ___, is that the truth, or a lie? [Young children equate truth with *fact*, lies with *non-fact*.]

6. Avoid the question of belief entirely (Do you believe that to be true?).

7. Avoid using the word "story." (Tell me your story in your own words.) "Story" means both "narrative account of a happening" and "fiction." Adults listening to adults take both meanings into consideration. Adults listening to children, however, might well hear "story" as only the latter. "Story" is not only an ambiguous concept, it can be prejudicial.

8. With children, redundancy in questions is a useful thing. Repeat names and places often instead of using strings of (often ambiguous) pronouns. Avoid unanchored "that"'s, and "there"'s. Give verbs all of their appropriate nouns (subjects and objects), as in "[I want you to] Promise *me* that *you* will tell *me* the truth," instead of "Promise me to tell the truth."

9. Watch your pronouns carefully (including "that"). Be sure they refer either to something you can physically point at, or to something in the very immediate (spoken) past, such as in the same sentence, or in the last few seconds.

10. In a related caution, be very careful about words whose meanings depend on their relation to the speaker and the immediate situation, such as personal pronouns (I, you, we), locatives (here, there), objects (this, that), and verbs of motion (come/go; bring/take).

11. Avoid tag questions (e.g., "You did it, *didn't you*?"). They are confusing to children. Avoid, too, Yes/No questions that are packed with lots of propositions. (Example of a bad simple-sounding question, with propositions numbered: "[1] Do you remember [2] when Mary asked you [3] if you knew [4] what color Mark's shirt was, and [5] you said, [6] 'Blue'?" What would a "Yes" or "No" answer tell you here?) It does not help the factfinder to rely on an answer if it's not clear what the question was.

12. See that the child stays firmly grounded in the appropriate questioning situation. If you are asking about the past, be sure the child understands that. If you shift to the present, make that clear too. If it's necessary to have the child recall a specific time/date/place in which an event occurred, keep reminding the child of the context of the questions. And don't use phrases like, "Let me direct your attention to." Try instead, "I want you to think back to...," or "Make a picture in your mind ...," or "I'm going to ask you some questions about...."

13. Explain to children why they are being asked the same questions more than once by more than one person. Repeated questioning is often interpreted (by adults as well as by children) to mean that the first answer was regarded as a lie, or wasn't the answer that was desired.

14. Be alert to the tendency of young children to be very literal and concrete in their language. "Did you have your *clothes* on?" might get a "No" answer; "Did you have your *p.j.'s* on?" might get a "Yes."

15. Don't *expect* children under about age 9 or 10 to give "reliable" estimates of time, speed, distance, size, height,

weight, color, or to have mastered any relational concept, including kinship. (Adults' ability to give many of these estimates is vastly overrated.)

16. Do not tell a child, "Just answer my question(s) yes or no." With their literal view of language, children can interpret this to mean that only a Yes or a No answer (or even "Yes or No"!) is permitted — period, whether or not such answers are appropriate. Under such an interpretation, children might think that answers like "I don't know/remember," and lawfully permitted explanations would be forbidden.

Appendix C: Some Basic Sentence-Building Principles For Talking to Children

Developed by Anne Graffam Walker, Ph.D.
Revised March 1999

1. Vocabulary

- Use words that are short (1-2 syllables) and common.

  Ex: "house" instead of "residence"

- Translate difficult words into easy phrases.

  Ex: "what happened to you" instead of "what you experienced"

- Use proper names and places instead of pronouns.

  Ex: "what did Marcy" do? instead of "what did she do?"; "in the house" instead of "in there"

- Use concrete, visualizable nouns ("back yard") instead of abstract ones ("area").

- Use verbs that are action-oriented.

  Ex: "point to," "tell me about," instead of "describe"

- Substitute simple, short verb forms for multi-word phrases when possible.

  Ex: "if you *went*" instead of "if you *were to have gone*"

- Use active voice for verbs instead of the passive.

  Ex: "Did you see a doctor?" instead of "Were you seen by a doctor?"

  [Note: One exception: the passive "get" ("Did you get hurt?"), which children acquire very early, and is easier to process than "Were you hurt?"]

2. Putting the words together

- · Aim for one main idea per question/sentence.

- · When combining ideas, introduce no more than one new idea at a time.

- · Avoid interrupting an idea with a descriptive phrase. Put the phrase (known as a relative clause) at the end of the idea instead.

  Ex: "Please tell me about the man *who had the red hat on*" instead of "The man *who had the red hat on* is the one I'd like you to tell me about."

- · Avoid difficult-to-process connectives like "while" and "during."

- · Avoid negatives whenever possible.

- · Avoid questions that give a child only 2 choices. Add an open-end choice at the end.

  Ex: "Was the hat red, or blue, or some other color?"

BOTTOM LINE: SHORT AND SIMPLE IS GOOD.

Appendix D. Prototype for Competency Voir Dire For Children

Developed by Anne Graffam Walker, Ph.D.[*]
Revised March 1999

The test for determining whether a child is competent to testify as a witness is well established in those states which require competency voir dire. It is typically expressed as follows:

The child must be found to have sufficient mental capacity to:

1) Observe the incident;

2) Remember the observed facts until the time of trial;

3) Communicate the observed data accurately at the trial;

4) Possess a consciousness of the duty to speak the truth (Charles E. Friend, The Law of Evidence in Virginia, 3d Ed. Sec 54)

What follows is a revised *prototype* for a voir dire which was first developed in 1990 as a response to judges' requests for some "language" with which to explore competency issues with children. Its intent is to provide assistance to judges and attorneys in assessing capacity in accordance with the above standards with minimal risk of confusing a child. These questions are designed to explore necessary legal concepts in age-appropriate language which children of normal cognitive and linguistic development, and general life experience, should be able to understand. They are offered, however with two caveats:

1) each child is different; and

2) the language used should fit the child and the situation.

---

* with grateful acknowledgment to Judge E. Preston Grissom for his assistance.

In recognition of varying degrees of cognitive and linguistic maturity in children, two versions of the questions are given. Format I is intended for children of elementary school age (7 - 12); Format II is for children age 6 and under, and can also be used for children of any age who appear to be confused, or frightened, or who have a developmental delay.

These questions, and the follow-up questions that appear in parentheses, are intended ONLY as a *GUIDE*; **they have not been tested empirically**, and it is not suggested that all of them are necessary in order to elicit essential responses. *Neither is it suggested that if a child is unable to provide answers for all of the questions, that child should be found incompetent.* It *is* suggested, however, that whatever personal deviations are made from this guide, an attempt be made to follow its model: grouping like topics together, introducing new topics as they arise so as to facilitate understanding, and using questions that are as short as possible, and words that are as simple as possible.

It may be worth mentioning here, too, that a child who is frightened, intimidated, or who has had no preparation for the experience of giving testimony, is less likely to be able to access his or her memory for past events. So a calm demeanor and tone of voice, even a smile, are more than cosmetic: they are tools for gaining information.

[NB: Questions in parentheses are suggested follow-ups.]

FORMAT I: Questions Designed to Explore Competency for Children of Elementary School Age

A. Capacity to Observe, Remember, and Communicate

1. [Appropriate greeting] My name is _____, and I am going to be asking you some questions. Let's start with your name: What is your name?
2. Will you spell your name for me, please?
3. Where do you live? (What is your address in [insert name of town/city...]?)
4. Do you live in a house, or an apartment, or what?
5. *OPTIONAL*: Tell me something about where you live – what it's like.
6. Did you live in some other house/apartment/X before this one?
   [*If Yes*: follow up with appropriate questions about where.]
7. Who lives in your house/apartment/X with you now?
8. What are their names?
9. Anyone else live there? [*If Yes*: Who?]
10. How old are you?
11. When were you born? when is your birthday?
12. Do you go to school? Where?
13. [*If home-schooled, go to #15; if not (and if necessary)*]:What's the name of the school?
14. How do you get to school every day?
15. What grade are you in?
16. Do you have a favorite subject in school – something you like to learn about best?
17. [*If Yes to #16*]: Tell me about it: Why is it your favorite?
    [*If No*]: No? Well then, tell me what you like to do when you aren't in school.

18. When you have a birthday, do you ever have a party, or do something special?

19. [*If Yes to #18*]: Do you remember what you did on your last birthday?
    [*If Yes*]: What did you do? Tell me everything you can remember about that day.
    [*If No*]: No? Well, how about if you tell me about some special day that you remember, like a holiday, or vacation, or something you did with your friends. Tell me as much as you can remember about that day. [Avoid mentioning religious holidays. Some families do not celebrate them.]

B. Consciousness of Duty to Speak the Truth

20. Let me ask you about something else now. Before you came to court, did someone talk to you about what to say? [*If Yes*]: What did he/she/they tell you?

21. [*If answer is a variation of "told me to tell the truth"*]: That's what I want to talk about: telling the truth and telling lies. [*Go to #22.*]
    [*If answer is something else, follow up appropriately.* Then]: What I want to talk to you about now is something very important: telling the truth and telling lies. [*Go on to 22.*]

22. Let me ask you something first. Who brought you here to court today?

23. So if someone said [**NB**: Do **Not** use, "If **I** said] that [child's answer] brought you here today, what is that: a lie, or the truth?

24. What if someone said that [someone else known to child/in courtroom/popular fictional character] brought you here? Is that the truth, a lie?

25. Is it a bad thing or is it a good thing to tell a lie?

26. Why is that?

27. What can happen when people tell lies?

28. Has your mom or your dad [other primary caretaker] talked to you about telling lies?
    [*If Yes*]: What did he/she/they tell you?

29. What happens at home if you tell a lie to your mom and dad/[other] and he/she finds out?
    [**NB**: Avoid asking if child has an idea of what could happen if he/she tells a lie in court.]

30. [*OPTIONAL*] What about at school? What happens there?

31. I have something else to ask you, [child's name]. Do you know what a promise is? [*Regardless of answer*]: If I promise you that I will do something for you, am I supposed to do it?

32. What about you? If you promise me that you will do something, are you supposed to do it?
    [*If Yes, move to #33. If some other answer, inquire*]: Tell me what you mean by that.

33. [*If applicable*]: A few minutes ago, the [bailiff/clerk/whoever] – that man/woman right over there – asked you to raise your right hand. And then he/she asked you if you would tell us the truth today. And you said, "Yes." When you said, "Yes," did you mean that you *promise* that you will tell the truth? [Avoid running these sentences together as you speak. Children need time to process.]
    [*If Yes*]: Will you do that?
    [*If some other answer*]: Tell me what you mean by that.

34. Let's talk for a minute about answering questions. If you don't know the answer to a question, do you know what to do?
    [*If Yes*]: What should you do? [If "Say I don't know"] Good. [*Go on to 2nd sentence in #35.*]
    [*If No, go on to #35.*]

35. Well, there's something I need to tell you about answers. When you don't know the answer to a question, you don't have to guess. It's O.K. for you to say, "I don't

know," if you really don't know. [Brief pause] And it's O.K. to say, "I don't remember," if you really don't remember. But it's not O.K. to guess, or to make something up. And it's not O.K. to say something that is not true.

Do you understand that? [Wait for answer.]

[*If Yes, continue; if No, go over rules again, then:*] O.K. Let me hear you tell me what the rules are here about guessing. And what about making something up? And if you don't remember?

[Wait for responses, and correct them, if necessary, or affirm if correct. This last step is *essential* in determining whether the child really understands what you've said.]

36. We're almost finished. Just a couple more questions. Do you know why you are here today, [child's name]?

    [*If Yes, inquire, and continue as in "No" answer.*]

    [*If No*]: Well, one thing you are here for today is to answer some questions [*if appropriate, continue*: about

    _____]. And another thing you are here for is to do a job. Everyone here today has a job to do, even you. Your job is to do what I just told you a minute ago: to tell the truth, and not guess. Your job is to answer all the questions the very best that you can. [Brief pause] And if you don't understand what the question means, you tell us, O.K.? We'll try to say it in different words.

37. O.K. Last questions: Will you promise me, [child's name] that you will tell the truth today, and not guess about anything? (Good.) And will you promise me that you won't tell any lies? (Good.)

FORMAT II: Questions Designed to Explore Competency for Children Below School Age*

*It is important to note a few things in connection with the questions suggested below.

- Pre-school children's ability to recite autobiographical facts (e.g., full name, age, address), their ability to recite cultural lists (e.g., numbers, the alphabet, days of the week, months of the year), or to do things like name colors, is largely dependent on the degree of exposure to these facts that the children have experienced in their everyday lives. Some parents are very active in teaching their children these things; some are not. In any case, the ability of children of *any* age, pre-school or not, to recite these lists is in no way connected to their ability to remember events accurately, *nor is it related to the ability to connect an act to a particular date, time, frequency, or duration.*

- There are a lot of questions here, and *they don't all have to be used*. A voir dire of this length may be particularly difficult for a 3-year-old. The younger the child, and the fewer the number of questions asked, the better. Young children's attention span is very short, and the longer that a voir dire goes on, the greater the likelihood for responses that don't reflect children's true competency.

- A word about the phrasing suggested in the following questions: You will notice that usually when you change a subject, I suggest that you do so explicitly ("Let's talk about X now..."). There are two reasons for that kind of framing: 1) naming the topic focuses attention; and 2) children are not as adept as adults at shifting from topic to topic mentally. You will also probably notice what seems to be a great deal of redundancy in the line of questions. Besides framing, redundancy increases the chance that you and the child will be talking about the same thing at the same time, which is, of course, essential if you expect to get accurate information. And so is *speaking slowly*. That includes not running several sentences/questions together as if they were one, especially with the younger children.

A. Capacity to Observe, Remember, and Communicate

1. [Appropriate greeting] My name is _____. What's your name? (Is that your whole name? What is your whole name?) [*If child is not familiar with "whole name"*]: Do you have some more names?

2. Do you have some brothers and sisters? (What are their names?)

3. What is your mother's/mommy's name? [*If answer is "Mommy", etc.*]: Does she have another name? [Pause] How about your dad/daddy? [**NB:** avoid "father"] What is his name?

4. Where do you live? [*If answer is something like "at home"*]: O.K. Do you know your address: like the name of the street you live on? [Wait for answer] How about the name of your town/city? Do you know that?) [*Don't expect answers to these address questions.*]

5. How old are you, [child's name]?

6. Do you know when your birthday is? (Prompt: Like in January, or February?)

7. What did you do on your last birthday? [*If child does not respond, move on to #8.*]

8. Did you do something special that day? [Pause] Tell me about your last birthday. I'd like to know about it. [*If child does not respond, move on to #9.*]

9. Let's talk a little bit about things you do every day. First, you get out of bed in the morning, don't you. What do you do next? [Pause] (Prompt: What happens at your house/apartment/ in the morning?)

10. Do you stay at home all day long?
[*If Yes*]: Who stays at home with you?

[*If No*]: Where do you go?

11. Do you watch T.V. sometimes?

12. Do you have a favorite T.V. show/program: one that you like the best? (What is it?)

13. What do you like about [name of program child mentions]?

14. Tell me something about that show/program. Who do you see on [name of the show]?

15. What happened on the last [name of program] that you saw? Do you remember? (Prompt: Like what did [insert any name/names the child has given you; or say "the people"] do?)
[*Do not expect full answers to these last three questions.*]

B. Consciousness of the Duty to Speak the Truth

16. Let me ask you something else now. You know you came here to talk to me/us about something important. Well, did someone tell you what to say? (What did he/she/they tell you?)

17. [*If answer is a variation of "told me to tell the truth"*]: O.K. That's what I want to talk about: telling the truth. [*Go to #18*].
[*If answer is something else, follow up appropriately.* Then]: What I want to talk to you about now is very important: I want to talk to you about telling what's real.
[*Go on to #18.*]

18. Let me ask you something first. Is it snowing in here?

19. So if someone says [*NOT "If I say"*] it's snowing in here, is that right/real/true, or wrong/not real/not true/a lie? [**NB**: *children 7 and under equate facts/reality to the truth, non-facts/unreality to a lie.*]

20. Is it a bad thing or a good thing to tell a lie?

21. What happens at home if you tell a lie to your mom or dad/other?

22. O.K.[child's name], now I want to talk to you for a minute about promises. **

      What if mom/dad promises to buy you some ice cream. What does that mean? [No pause] Is she/he *supposed* to buy you ice cream, or what? [You may get some answers here about real life actions on the part of parents that will show you clearly that children understand, "But you *promised!*"]

23. Well, what about me? If I promise you that I will do something *for sure*, am I supposed to do it?

24. And what about you? If *you* promise *me* that you will do something for sure, are you supposed to do it?
      [*If the child says "No" to #23 or #24, follow up with*]: No? Tell me about that.

25. [*Only if applicable; otherwise, move to #26*]: A few minutes ago, that man/woman over there [point] asked you to raise your hand. And then he/she asked you if you would tell us the truth today. And you said "Yes," didn't you? [Pause] Well, when you said "Yes," that was like a promise that you'd only tell us what really happened. So will you do that? [Pause] Will you tell us only things you know *for sure*? [Respond appropriately] And you won't tell us any lies? (Good.)

26. Now, let me ask you something else: What do you think, [child's name]? Do I have a dog at my house?

** **The word "promise" can be** *used* **in ways that are very difficult for young persons to process.** One use that can give children, even school-age children, a problem is found in the question that some judges feel they must ask: "Has anyone promised you anything for coming here today?" That wording uses a somewhat abstract verb form (has promised), and leaves out the essential phrase "to give" (promised *to give* you). If such a question is absolutely necessary, try phrasing it as follows: "Did someone promise to give you something special/good/that you'd like [very brief pause] for coming here today?" Or avoid the word "promise" by asking: "Did someone [not "anyone"] tell you that you'd get something special for coming here today?"

[*If answer is* , "*I don't know*"]: That's a good [**not** "right"] answer, because you really don't know. So if we ask you a question, and you don't know the answer, what are you going to say?

[*If child responds, "I don't know"*]: Good.

[*If child doesn't respond, say again*]: You're going to say, "I don't know, O.K.? (Good.)

[*If answer is "Yes" or "No," regardless of whether the answer is correct or not*]: How did you know that? [Pause, and then adapt following to response]: Well, I'll bet you guessed. Sometimes, we guess when we really don't know the answer. But today, we don't want you to guess. O.K.? [Pause] And we don't want you to make anything up. You don't have to. [Pause] Just tell us what you really know. That's what we want to hear. [Pause] So if you don't know something, just say, "I don't know." That's an O.K. answer. Will you do that? [Respond appropriately.]

27. Do you know why you are here today, [child's name]? [*If Yes, inquire. Whether response is Yes or No, continue with #28*].

28. Did you know that you have a job to do here today? [No pause] Your job is to do what we just talked about. Your job is to tell the truth. [Pause] And your job is to say, "I don't know" if you really don't know. [Short pause] Or you can say, 'I don't remember" if you really don't remember. Will you do that? (Good.)

29. O.K. One more thing, [child's name], and then I'm all done. We talked about promises a minute ago. So I need to ask you: Will you *promise* that you will tell the truth today for sure? You will tell us just what was real? [Pause] And you promise that you won't tell any lies? [Pause] (That's good. Thank you.)

[**NB:** Research indicates that young children regard "will" as placing more obligation on them to tell the truth than "promise." Therefore, it is recommended that you use both "will" and "promise," as written above.]

References

Abbeduto, L., & Rosenberg, S. (1985). Children's knowledge of the presuppositions of *know* and other cognitive verbs. *Journal of Child Language, 12*, 621-641.

Abney, Veronica (Winter,1999). Understanding child sexual abuse in the African-American Community. *The National Child Advocate*, 2:3, 4-5, 10-12.

Baladerian, N. (1993, December). *Getting acquainted with children with disabilities.* Presentation to the Tenth National Conference on Child Abuse & Neglect. Pittsburgh, PA.

Basso, K. (1972). 'To give up on words': Silence in Western Apache Culture. In P. Giglioli (Ed.), *Language and social context*, pp. 67-86. New York: Penguin Books.

Beck, M. (1982). Kidspeak. *How your child develops language skills*. New York: New American Library.

Berk, L. (1997). *Child Development*, 4th Ed. Boston: Allyn and Bacon.

Berlin, B. & Kay, P. (1969). *Basic color terms: Their universality and evolution*. Berkeley and Los Angeles: University of California Press.

Berliner, L., & Barbieri, M. (1984). The testimony of the child victim of sexual assault. *Journal of Social Issues, 40*, 125-137.

Bernstein, B. (1972). Social class, language and socialization. In P. Giglioli (Ed.), *Language and social context*, pp.157-178. New York: Penguin Books.

Bloom, L. (1991). *Language development from two to three.* New York: Cambridge University Press.

Boggs, S., & Eyberg, S. (1990). Interview techniques and establishing rapport. In A. LaGreca (Ed.), *Through the eyes of the child: Obtaining self-reports from children and adolescents*, pp. 85-108. Boston, MA: Allyn and Bacon.

Bolinger, D. & Sears, D. (1981). *Aspects of Language, 3rd Ed.* New York: Harcourt Brace Jovanovich, Inc.

Bonitatibus, G., Godshall, S., Kelley, M., Levering, T., & Lynch, E. (1988). The role of social cognition in comprehension monitoring. *First Language, 8,* 287-298.

Bowerman, M. (1988). Inducing the latent structure of language. In F. Kessel (Ed.), *The development of language and language researchers: Essays in honor of Roger Brown,* pp. 23-49. Hillsdale, NJ: Lawrence Erlbaum.

Brennan, M., & Brennan, R. (1988). *Strange language,* 3rd Ed. Wagga-Wagga, N.S.W.: Charles Sturt University-Riverina.

Brown, R. (1973). *A first language.* Cambridge, MA: Harvard University Press.

Brown, R. (1988). Form and meaning in early language. In M. Franklin & S. Barten (Eds.), *Child language: A reader,* pp. 75-88. New York: Oxford University Press.

Brown, R., & Lennenberg, E. (1958). Studies in linguistic relativity. In E. Maccoby (Ed.), *Readings in Social Psychology,* 3rd ed., pp. 9-18. New York: Rinehart & Winston.

Burton, R. & Strichartz, A. (1992). Liar! Liar! Pants afire! In S. Ceci, M. Leichtman, & M. Putnick (Eds.), *Cognitive and social factors in early deception,* pp. 11-28. Hillsdale, NJ: Erlbaum

Carter, C. (1992). *The effects of linguistic complexity and social support on children's reports.* Unpublished doctoral dissertation, State University of New York at Buffalo, Buffalo, New York.

Carter, C., Bottoms, B., & Levine, M. (1996). Linguistic and socioemotional influences on the accuracy of children's reports. *Law and Human Behavior, 20:*3, 335-358.

Chambers, J., & Tavuchis, N. (1975). Kids and kin: Children's understanding ofAmerican kin terms. *Journal of Child Language, 3,* 63-80.

Chan, S. (1992). Families with Asian roots. In Lynch, E. & Hanson, M. (Eds.), *Developing cross-cultural competence,* pp. 181-257. Baltimore, MD: Paul Brookes Publishing Company.

Chandler, M., Fritz, A., & Hala, S. (1989). Small scale deceit: Deception as a marker of two-, three-, and four-year-olds' early theories of mind. *Child Development, 60,* 1263-1277.

Charney, R. (1980). Speech roles and the development of personal pronouns. *Journal of Child Language, 7*, 509-528.

Charrow, R., & Charrow, V. (1979). Making legal language understandable: A psycholinguistic study of jury instructions. *Columbia Law Review, 79*, 1306-1374.

Chomsky, C. (1969). *The acquisition of syntax in children from 5 to 10.* Cambridge, MA: The M.I.T. Press.

Clark, E. (1971). On the acquisition of the meaning of before and after. *Journal of Verbal Learning and Verbal Behavior, 10*, 266-275.

Clark, E. & Garnica, O. (1974). Is he coming or going? On the acquisition of deictic verbs. *Journal of Verbal Learning and Verbal Behavior, 13*, 559-72.

Clark, H. & Clark, E. (1977). *Psychology and language.* New York: Harcourt Brace Jovanovich.

Collins, W., Wellman, H., Keniston, A., & Westby, S. (1978). Age-related aspects of comprehension and inferences from a televised dramatic narrative. *Child Development, 49*, 389-399.

Copen, L. (1996). *Children's thoughts about court-related words.* Unpublished paper.

Cross, T. (1992, February). *Cultural competency issues in child welfare services.* Presentation at the Eighth National Symposium on Child Sexual Abuse, Huntsville, AL.

Danet, B., Hoffman, K., Kermish, N., Rafn, H., & Stayman, D. (1980). An ethnography of questioning in the courtroom. In R. Shuy & A. Shnukal (Eds.), *Language use and the uses of language*, pp. 222-233. Washington, D.C.: Georgetown University Press.

Davies, E. & Seymour, F.(1997). Child witnesses in the criminal courts: Furthering New Zealand's commitment to the United Nations Convention on the Rights of the Child. *Psychiatry, Psychology and Law, 4*, 1 (April): 13-24.

deVilliers, J., & deVilliers, P. (1974). Competence and performance in child language: Are children really competent to judge? *Journal of Child Language, 1*, pp.11-21.

deVilliers, J., & deVilliers, P. (1978). *Language acquisition*. Cambridge, MA: Harvard University Press.

Eisenberg, A. (1985). Learning to describe past experiences in conversation. *Discourse Processes, 8*, 177-204.

Elkind, D. (1978). *The child's reality*. Hillsdale, NJ: Lawrence Erlbaum.

Felker, D., (Ed.), (1980). *Document design: A review of the relevant research*. Washington, D.C.: American Institutes for Research.

Fivush, R. (1993). Developmental perspectives on autobiographical recall. In G. Goodman & B. Bottoms (Eds.), *Child victims, child witnesses: Understanding and improving testimony*, pp 1-24. New York: Guilford Press.

Fivush, R. (1993). Developmental perspectives on autobiographical recall. In G. Goodman & B. Bottoms (Eds.), *Child victims, child witnesses: Understanding and improving testimony*, pp 1-24 . New York: Guildford Press.

Fivush, R., Gray, J., & Fromhoff, F. (1987). Two year olds talk about the past. *Cognitive Development, 2*, 393-410.

Fivush, R., & Shukat, J. (1995). Content, consistency and coherency of early autobiographical recall. In M. Zaragoza, J. Graham, G. Hall, R. Hirschman, & Y. Ben-Porath (Eds.), *Memory and testimony in the child witness*, pp. 5-23. Thousand Oaks, CA: Sage.

Fraser, C., Bellugi, U., & Brown, R. (1963). Control of grammar in imitation, comprehension, and production. *Journal of Verbal Behavior, 2*, 121-135.

French, L.A., & Nelson, K. (1985). *Young children's knowledge of relationship terms. Some if's, or's, and buts*. New York: Springer-Verlag.

Friedman, W. (1982). Conventional time concepts and children's structuring of time. In W. Friedman, (Ed.), *The developmental psychology of time*, pp. 171-208. New York: Academic Press.

Gallagher, T. (1977). Revision behaviors in the speech of normal children developing language. *Journal of Speech and Hearing Research, 20*, 303-318.

Garbarino, J., Stoot, F., and Faculty of The Erikson Institute. (1992). *What children can tell us: Eliciting, interpreting, and evaluating critical information from children.* San Francisco: Jossey-Bass.

Gelman, R., Meck, E., & Merkin, S. (1986). Young children's numerical competence. *Cognitive Development, 1,* 1-29.

Goodman, G., Aman, C., & Hirschman, J. (1987). Child sexual and physical abuse: Children's testimony. In S. Ceci, M. Toglia, & D. Ross, (Eds.), *Children's eyewitness memory,* pp.1-23. New York: Springer-Verlag.

Goodman, G., & Clark-Stewart, A. (1991). Suggestibility in children's testimony: Implications for sexual abuse investigations. In J. Doris, (Ed.), *The suggestibility of children's recollections: Implications for eyewitness testimony,* pp. 92-105. Washington, D.C.: American Psychological Association.

Goodz, N. (1982). Is before really easier to understand than after? *Child Development, 53,* 822-825.

Gumperz, J. (1977). Sociocultural knowledge in conversational inference. In M. Saville-Troike (Ed.), *Georgetown University Round Table on Languages and Linguistics.* Washington, D.C.: Georgetown University School of Languages and Linguistics.

Gumperz, J. (1982). Fact and inference in courtroom testimony. In J. Gumperz (Ed.), *Language and social identity,* pp.163-195. New York: Cambridge University Press.

Hall, W., & Nagy, W. (1979, October). *Theoretical issues in the investigation of words of internal report* (Tech. Rep. No. 146). Urbana: University of Illinois, Center for the Study of Reading.

Heath, S. (1983). *Ways with words: Language, life, and work in communities and classrooms.* New York: Cambridge University Press.

Hewitt, S. (1999). *Assessing preschool children with allegations of abuse.* Thousand Oaks, CA: Sage Publications, Inc.

Hill, R., Collis, G., & Lewis, V. (1997). Young children's understanding of the cognitive verb *forget. Journal of Child Language, 24,* 57-79.

Horgan, D. (1978). The development of the full passive. *Journal of Child Language, 5*, 65-80.

Hudson, J., Gebelt, J., Haviland, J., & Bentivegna, C. (1992). Emotion and narrative structure in young children's personal accounts. *Journal of Narrative and Life History, 2*, 129-150.

Huffman, M., Warren, A., & Frazier, S. (1998). *Truth/lie discussions in sexual abuse interviews with children: "The truth or not the truth?"* Paper presented at the American Psychology-Law Society Meeting, Redondo Beach, CA.

— Hunt, J., Komori, L., Kellen, L., Galas, J., & Gleason,T. (1995). Faulty and non-productive questioning techniques: Potential pitfalls of the child interview. Paper presented in N. Perry (Chair), *Communicating with child witnesses: current practices and future directions.* Symposium at the Meeting of the Society for Applied Research in Memory and Cognition, Vancouver, B.C., Canada.

Joe, J. & Malach, R. (1992). Families with Native American roots. In Lynch, E. & Hanson, M., *Developing cross-cultural competence*, pp. 89-118. Baltimore, MD: Paul Brookes Publishing Company.

Johnson, C. & Wellman, H. (1980). Children's developing understanding of mental verbs: Remember, know, and guess. *Child Development, 51*, 1095-1102.

Kail, R. (1991). Developmental change in speed of processing during childhood and adolescence. *Psychological Bulletin, 109*:3, 490-501.

Kessel, F. (1970). The role of syntax in children's comprehension from ages 6-12. *Monograph of the Society for Research in Child Development, 35.*

Kessel, F. (1988). *Development of Language and Language Researchers: Essays in honor of Roger Brown.* Hillsdale, NJ: Erlbaum Associates.

Labov, W. (1972). *Language in the inner city.* Philadelphia: University of Pennsylvania Press.

Labov, W., & Waletsky J. (1967). Narrative analysis: Oral versions of personal experience. In J. Helm (Ed.), *Essays on the verbal and visual arts*, pp.12-44. Seattle: University of Washington Press.

Lane, C. (1984). Mis-communication between native and second-language speakers of English. In A. Berry (Ed.), *Communication*, pp 1-12. Auckland: Primary Principals Association.

Lieberman, P. (1963). Some effects of semantic and grammatical context on the production and perception of speech. In *Language and Speech, 6,* 172-187.

Lynch, E. & Hanson, J. *Developing cross-cultural competence.* Baltimore, MD: Paul Brookes Publishing Company.

Lyon, T., & Flavell, J. (1994). Young children's understanding of "remember" and "forget." *Child Development, 65,* 1357-1371.

Lyon, T., Kaplan, D., Dorado, J., & Saywitz, K. Young maltreated and non-referred children's understanding that promising increases the likelihood of performance. Manuscript in preparation.

Lyon, T. & Saywitz, K. 1999. Young maltreated children's competence to take the oath. *Applied Developmental Science, 3,* 16-27.

Lund, N., & Duchan, J. (1993). *Assessing children's language in naturalistic contexts,* 3rd Ed. Englewood Cliffs, NJ: Prentice-Hall.

Macias v. State, 776 S.W.2d 255 (Tx.App.1989).

Mandler, J., & Johnson, N. (1977). Remembrance of things parsed: Story structure and recall. *Cognitive Psychology, 9,* 111-151.

Markman, E. (1979). Realizing that you don't understand: Elementary school children's awareness of inconsistencies. *Child Development, 50,* 643-655.

Mellinkoff, D. (1963). *The language of the law.* Boston, MA: Little, Brown and Company.

Memon, A, & Vartoukian, R. (1996). The effects of repeated questioning on young children's eyewitness testimony. *British Journal of Psychology, 87*, 403-415.

Michaels, S., & Collins, J. (1984). Oral discourse styles: Classroom interaction and the acquisition of literacy. In D. Tannen (Ed.), *Coherence in spoken and written discourse*, pp. 219-244. Norwood, NJ: Ablex.

Mitchell, P., & Robinson, E. (1992). Children's understanding of the evidential connotation of 'know' in relation to overestimation of their own knowledge. *Journal of Child Language, 19*, 167-182.

Moore, A., Bergman, P., & Binder, D. 1996. *Trial advocacy: Inferences, arguments, & techniques* (American Casebook Series). West Information Publishing Group.

Moore, C., & Furrow, D. (1991). The development of the language of belief: The expression of relative certainty. In D. Frye & C. Moore, (Eds.), *Children's theories of mind: Mental states and social understanding*. Hillsdale, NJ: Lawrence Erlbaum.

Morrill, A. (1976). *Trial diplomacy*. Chicago: Court Practice Institute.

Morrow, P. (1992). *Communicative style and judicial outcomes in a cross-cultural setting*. Paper prepared for the 1992 Law and Society Annual Meeting.

Nippold, M. (1988). Linguistic ambiguity. In M. Nippold, (Ed.), *Later language development: Ages nine through nineteen*, pp. 211-223. Boston, MA: College- Hill Press.

Okamura, A., Heras, P., & Wong-Kerberg, L. (1995). Asian, Pacific Island, and Filipino Americans and Sexual Child Abuse. In Fontes, L. (Ed.), *Sexual abuse in nine North American cultures: Treatment and prevention*, pp. 67-96. Thousand Oaks, CA: Sage Publications.

Olson, D., & Astington, J. (1986). Children's acquisition of metalinguistic and metacognitive verbs. In W. Demopoulous & A. Marras, (Eds.), *Language learning and concept acquisition: Foundational issues*, pp. 184-199. Norwood, NJ: Ablex.

Pease, D., Berko Gleason, J., & Pan, B. (1993). Learning the meaning of words: Semantic development and beyond. In J. Berko Gleason (Ed.), *The development of language*, 3rd Ed., pp. 115-150. New York: Macmillan.

Perner, J., Leekam, S., & Wimmer, H. (1986). *The insincerity of conservation questions: Children's growing insensitivity to experimenter's intentions.* Unpublished manuscript. University of Sussex.

Perry, N. (1995). Children's comprehension of truths, lies, and false beliefs. In T. Ney (Ed.), *True and false allegations in child sexual abuse: Assessment and case management.* New York: Brunner/Mazel.

— Perry, N., Claycomb, L., Tam, P., McAuliff, B., Dostal, C., & Flanagan, C. (1993, March). *When lawyers question children: Is justice served?* Paper presented to the Biennial Meeting of the Society for Research in Child Development, New Orleans.

Perry, N., Kern, S., Eitemiller, J., Mohn, S., Fischer, M., & Stessman, L. (n.d). *Factors affecting children's ability to provide accurate testimony.* Unpublished manuscript.

— Perry, N., & Teply, L. (1985). Interviewing, counseling, and in-court examination of children: Practical approaches for attorneys. *Creighton Law Review, 18,* 1369-1426.

— Perry, N., & Wrightsman, L. (1991). *The child witness.* Newbury Park, CA: Sage.

Peterson, C. (1990). The who, when and where of early narratives. *Journal of Child Language, 17,* 433-455.

Phinney, M. (1981). Children's interpretation of negation in complex sentences. In S. Tavakolian, (Ed.), *Language acquisition and linguistic theory.* Cambridge, MA: The M.I.T. Press.

Piaget, J. (1932/1965). *The moral judgement of the child.* New York: Free Press.

Poole, D. & Lamb, M. (1998). *Investigative interviews of children: A guide for helping professionals.* Washington, D.C.: American Psychological Association.

Poole, D., & Lindsay, D. (1995). Cognitive development. In R. Bull (Ed.), Unit 1 (Relevant aspects of development. *Distance learning post-graduate diploma course in child forensic studies: Psychology and law*.) Great Britain: Universities of Lees, Liverpool, and Portsmouth.

Quirk, R., Greenbaum, S., Leech, G., & Swartik, J. (1985). *A comprehensive grammar of the English Language*. London: Longman.

Reich, P. (1986). *Language development*. Englewood Cliffs, NJ: Prentice-Hall.

Reese, E. & Fivush, R. (1993). Parental styles of talk about the past. *Developmental Psychology, 29*, 596-606.

Richards, M. (1982). Empiricism and learning to mean. In S. Kuczaj II, (Ed.), *Language development, Vol. 1: Syntax and semantics*, pp.365-396. Hillsdale, NJ: Lawrence Erlbaum.

Richardson, G. (1989). *Talking to abused children: What attorneys need to know*. Unpublished ms.

Romaine, S. (1984). *The language of children and adolescents: The acquisition of communicative competence*. London: Basil Blackwell.

Saywitz, K. (1989). Court is a place to play basketball: Children's conceptions of the legal system. In S. Ceci, D. Ross, & M. Toglia, *Perspectives on children's testimony*, pp. 131-157. New York: Springer-Verlag.

Saywitz, K. (1995). Improving children's testimony: The question, the answer, and the environment. In M. Zaragoza, J. Graham, G.C.N. Hall, R. Hirschman & Y. Ben-Porath (Eds.), *Memory and testimony in the child witness*, pp.113-140. Thousand Oaks, CA: Sage.

Saywitz, K., Jaenicke, C., & Camparo, L. (1990). Children's knowledge of legal terminology. *Law & Human Behavior, 14*, 523-535.

Saywitz, K. & Lyon, D. (1997). *Sensitively assessing children's testimonial competence*. (Final report to the National Center on Child Abuse and Neglect, Grant No. 90-CA-1553).

Saywitz, K., & Nathanson, R. (1993). Children's testimony and their perceptions of stress in and out of the courtroom. *The International Journal of Child Abuse and Neglect, 17,* 613-622.

Saywitz, K., & Snyder, L. (1993). Improving children's testimony with preparation. In G. Goodman, & B. Bottoms (Eds.), *Child victims, child witnesses: Understanding and improving testimony,* pp. 117-146. New York: The Guilford Press.

— Saywitz, K., & Snyder, L. (1996). Narrative elaboration: Test of a new procedure for interviewing children. *Journal of Consulting and Clinical Psychology, 64,* 1347-1357.

—Saywitz, K., Snyder, L., & Lamphear, V. (1996). Helping children tell what happened: Follow-up study of the narrative elaboration procedure. *Child Maltreatment, 1:*200-212.

Siegal, M. (1991). *Knowing children: Experiments in conversation and cognition.* Hillsdale, NJ: Lawrence Erlbaum.

Siegler, R. (1991). *Children's thinking,* 2nd Ed. Englewood Cliffs, NJ: Prentice-Hall.

State v. Brovold, 477 N.W.2d 775 (Mn.App.1991).

State v. Ward, 619 N.E.2d 1119 (Oh.App.1992).

Stein, N., & Glenn, C. (1979). An analysis of story comprehension in elementary school children. In R. Freedle (Ed.), *New directions in discourse processing* (Vol. 2, pp. 53-120). Norwood, NJ: Ablex.

Strichartz, A. & Burton, R. (1990). Lies and truth: A study of the development of the concept. *Child Development, 61,* 211-220.

Strickland v. State, 550 So.2d1042 (Ala.Crim.App.1988).

Tager-Flusberg, H. (1993). Putting words together: Morphology and syntax in the pre-school years. In J. Berko Gleason (Ed.), *The development of language,* 3rd Ed., pp. 151-193. New York: Macmillan.

Tannen, D. (1985) Silence: Anything but. In M. Saville-Troike (Ed.), *Perspectives on Silence.* pp. 93-112. Norwood, NJ: Ablex.

Vurpillot, E., & Ball, W. (1979). The concept of identity and children's selective attention. In G. Hale & M. Lewis (Eds.), *Attention and cognitive development*, pp. 23-42. New York: Plenum.

Walker, A.(n.d.) Unpublished research. *In front of: a preposition that can be interpreted in different ways even by adults.*

Walker, A. (1982). Discourse rights of witnesses: Their circumscription in trial. *Sociolinguistic Working Paper No. 95*, Austin, TX: Southwest Educational Development Laboratory.

Walker, A. (1985). The two faces of silence: The effect of witness hesitancy on lawyers' impressions. In D. Tannen, & M. Saville-Troike (Eds.), *Perspectives on silence*, pp. 55-75. Norwood, NJ: Ablex.

Walker, A. (1987). Linguistic manipulation, power, and the legal setting. In L. Kedar (Ed.), *Power through discourse*, pp. 57-80. Norwood, NJ: Ablex.

Walker, A. (1990, November). *How to interview children and help them be good witnesses.* Co-presentation with John E.B. Myers at the ABA Fifth National Conference on Children and the Law, Washington, D.C.

Walker, A. (1993). Questioning young children in court: A linguistic case study. *Law and Human Behavior, 17,* 59-81.

Walker, A. (1999). Children in the courts: When language gets in the way. *Trial, 35:1,* January, pp. 50-53.

Walker, A. & McKinley-Pace, M. (1995, July). *"Do you know the difference between the truth and a lie?": An incompetent competency question.* Paper presented at the 1st Biennial Meeting of the Society for Applied Research in Memory and Cognition. University of British Columbia, Vancouver, B.C.

Walker, A. & Warren, A. (1995). The language of the child abuse interview: Asking the questions, understanding the answers. In T. Ney, (Ed.), *Allegations in child sexual abuse: Assessment and case management.* New York: Brunner/Mazel.

Walker, N. (1997, April 6). Should we question how we question children in child abuse investigations? In M. Bruck & H. Hembrooke (Chairs), *Beyond suggestibility: Interviews, interviewers, and the information they elicit from children.* Symposium presented at the biennial meeting of the Society for Research in Child Development, Washington, D.C.

Walker, N., & Hunt, J. (1998). Interviewing child victim-witnesses: What you ask is what you get. In C. Thompson, D. Hermann, J. Read, D. Bruce, D. Payne, and M.Toglia (Eds.), *Eyewitness memory: Theoretical and applied perspectives,* pp. 55-87. Mahwah, NJ: Erlbaum.

Walker, N., & Nguyen, M. (1996). Interviewing the child witness: The do's and the don'ts, the how's and the why's. *Creighton Law Review, 29:4,* 1587-1617.

Warren, A., & McCloskey, L. (1993). Pragmatics: Language in social contexts. In J. Berko Gleason (Ed.), *The development of language* 3rd Ed., pp. 195-237. New York: Macmillan.

Warren, A. & McGough, L. (1996). Research on children's suggestibility: Implications for the investigative interview. *Criminal Justice and Behavior, 23:2,* June, pp. 269-303.

Warren-Leubecker, A., Tate, C., Hinton, I., & Ozbek, I. (1989). What do children know about the legal system and when do they know it? First steps down a less traveled path to child witness research. In S. Ceci, D. Ross, & M. Toglia, (Eds.), *Perspectives on children's testimony,* pp. 158-183. New York: Springer-Verlag.

Watson-Gegeo, K., & Boggs, S. (1977). From verbal play to talk story: The role of routines in speech events among Hawaiian children. In S. Ervin-Tripp & C. Mitchell-Kernan (Eds.), *Child Discourse,* pp. 67-90. New York: Academic Press, Inc.

Wellman, H. & Johnson, C. (1979). Understanding of mental processes: A developmental study of *remember* and *forget. Child Development, 50,* 79-88.

Whitehurst, G. (1976). The development of communication changes with age and modeling. *Child Development, 47,* 473-482.

Wigglesworth, G. (1990). Children's narrative acquisition: A study of some aspects of reference and anaphora. *First Language*, 10, 105-125.

Wimmer, H., Gruber, S., & Perner, J. (1984). Young children's conception of lying: Moral intuition and the denotation and connotation of to lie. *Developmental Psychology*, 21, 993-995.

Wood, B. (1981). *Children and communication: Verbal and nonverbal language development*, 2nd Ed. Englewood Cliffs, NJ: Prentice-Hall.

Woodbury, H. (1984). The strategic use of questions in court. *Semiotica*, 48, 197-228.

Author Index

Subject Index

G

H

I

J